Thomas Knox

Thomas Knox's Business and Family Directory of Springfield,

Illinois, for 1881-82

Thomas Knox

Thomas Knox's Business and Family Directory of Springfield, Illinois, for 1881-82

ISBN/EAN: 9783337370251

Printed in Europe, USA, Canada, Australia, Japan

Cover: Foto ©ninafisch / pixelio.de

More available books at **www.hansebooks.com**

THOMAS KNOX'S

BUSINESS

AND

FAMILY DIRECTORY

OF

SPRINGFIELD, ILLINOIS,

FOR 1881--82.

———◆———

SPRINGFIELD:
H. W. ROKKER, PRINTER AND BINDER.
1881.

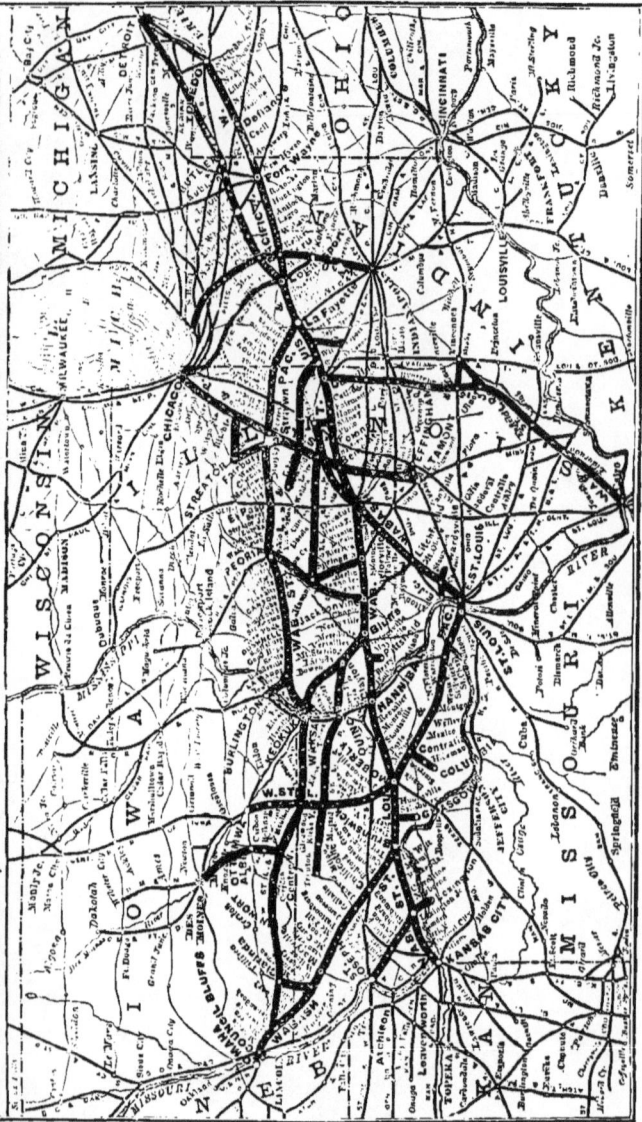

MAP OF THE

WABASH, ST. LOUIS & PACIFIC RAILWAY.

Look at the above Map, and you will see that the

WABASH, ST. LOUIS AND PACIFIC RAILWAY

—— IS THE——

Shortest Route for you to go, both East and West.

3,300 MILES OF ROAD!

Splendid Dining Cars attached to all Trains.

The Best THROUGH CAR LINE out of Springfield.

BAGGAGE CHECKED TO ALL IMPORTANT POINTS.

☞ *For any information call on or address*

H. C. TOWNSEND,
General Passenger Agent,

GEORGE H. DANIELS,
General Freight Agent,

} St. Louis, Mo.

THEO. McEUEN,
Ticket Agent,
Springfield, Ill.

INTRODUCTION.

— —

HIS BOOK is the result of the labors of a man who has lived more than a quarter of a century continuously in Springfield, and has consequently seen it more than treble in population, wealth, railroad facilities, manufacturing enterprises, and all that goes to make it a desirable place of residence and for business. The fact that he knows personally, and is known to, one or more in almost every family in the city and its suburbs, has been an important factor in obtaining accurate and complete information.

He takes pleasure in the reflection that he is not under the necessity of going from home to have his work done, but that the printing and binding attests the skill of Springfield workmen, thus making it wholly a home production. In this he sets an example worthy of imitation by all. If every citizen would do all he could to have every article sold here manufactured here, we would soon have a city of half a million inhabitants. We have inexhaustible mines of coal, and may have an equal supply of water by displaying the proper enterprise. We have railroads radiating to more than twice the cardinal points of the compass. We have street railroads reaching from the center to all parts of the circumference of the city, with many other advantages not necessary here to enumerate. We are in the center of a large area of the richest country on the globe, and can feed, with all the staples of life, armies of operatives. We have a successful watch factory and an iron mill, each on a mammoth scale, with a woolen mill, paper mill, machine shops, printing offices, etc., etc. Why not have cotton mills, plow factories, boot and shoe factories, furniture factories, with thousands of others, even to the seemingly insignificant pins and needles, but really gigiantic on account of the enormous numbers used by high and low, rich and poor? Here is the place to sell. Why not manufacture here, and by that means have something to sell?

A FRIEND TO THE

COMPILER AND PUBLISHER.

HISTORICAL.

SPRINGFIELD, one of the brightest gems in the crown of the proud Sucker State, is one of the most beautiful cities in the broad West. But a few years ago Springfield was a small, steady-going old fogy town, while to-day she is a live, bright, rushing city, onward and upward on her resistless march. Situated in the richest portion of the great State of Illinois, with a most cultivated, enterprising population, the seat of culture and refinement, there is nothing too bright or too promising for her in the near future. With the iron arms of over a half dozen railroads reaching out like vast arteries through the city, bringing to us the marvelous grain products of the rich Prairie State, we find our marts are busy and full of life. A few short years ago the Capital City was a wild, barren waste; to-day her inhabitants number over thirty thousand. Among the many advantages presented by the Capital City, none is greater than her system of public schools. The educational advantages of Springfield, both public and private, cannot be excelled, and in enumerating her riches, she may well exclaim, as she points to her tall and stately school houses, "These are my jewels." The manufacturing interests of Springfield are very large, and constantly growing. Among the numerous large establishments must be mentioned our magnificent Rolling Mill, one of the largest in the Western country, and whose operations are of such magnitude as to almost surpass belief. The Watch Factory is another vast establishment, constantly growing, and giving employment to an almost countless army of opertives, whilst its products rank with the very highest and best. A large and perfectly equipped Woolen Mill does an enormous business, while a Powder Mill, Plow Factory and an enormous Cotton Mill will soon be numbered with the gigantic manufacturing enterprises of our city.

With the best coal in the country at our very doors, with unexcelled railroad facilities, no city can offer stronger and better inducements to the capitalist to invest his surplus cash in manufacturing. Street cars penetrate nearly every part of the city —

whilst new lines will soon be completed. Our Fire Department has no superior in the whole State; our Flour Mills the best in the country, whilst the religious and educational interest of the Capital are indeed worthy of emulation and commendation.

Finally, with the many advantages Springfield can offer, there is no point in our broad domain more worthy the attention or presenting better inducements as a home for the capitalist, the artizan or the cosmopolite, than the object of this sketch, the beautiful Capital of the Sucker State.

STREET DIRECTORY.

First street is the dividing line between East and West. Beginning with No. 100 on the southeast corner of First and Washington, numbering East to Avenue, 1830, (18 blocks.) On the southwest corner of First and Washington, No. 100, going West to 934. On the northeast corner of First and Washington, No. 101 East to 1831. The numbers on the south side of all the East and West streets are EVEN and on the North side ODD. The North and South streets number each way from Washington street, EVEN numbers East side and on ODD numbers on West side.

LOCATION OF STREET LETTER BOXES.

N.E. Cor. 6th and Washington.
" " 5th and Madison.
" " 8th and Jefferson.
" " 10th and Washington.
" " 11th and Jefferson.
" " 12th and Madison.
" " 7th and Mason.
" " 6th and Reynolds.
" " 7th and Carpenter.
" " 9th and Miller.
" " 10th and Carpenter.
" " 5th and Washington.
    Revere House.
" " 3d and Jefferson.
    St. Nicholas Hotel.
    Court House.
North 5th bet. Madison and
    Carpenter.
Corner 5th and Union.
" 4th and Carpenter.
" 2d and Washington.
" 2d and Mason.
" Mason and Rutlege.
" 1st and Union.
" 5th and Monroe.
" 5th and Adams.
    State House.
" College and Monroe.
" College and Cook.

Corner Edwards and Spring.
" Wright and Second.
" 4th and Jackson.
" 5th and Wright.
" 15th and Washington.
" 17th and Capitol Av.
" 14th and Edwards.
" 11th and Clay.
    Wabash Shops.
" 7th and Allen.
" 6th and Scarritt.
" 5th and Allen.
" Spring and Scarritt.
" Governor and Walnut.
" Jefferson and Walnut.
" 5th and Elm.
" 6th and Keys' Av.
    Leland Hotel.
" 6th and Adams.
" 8th and Monroe.
" 8th and Jackson.
" 11th and Jackson.
" 13th and Monroe.
" 12th and Capitol Av.
" 12th and Douglas.
" 19th and Cook.
" 6th and Cook.
" 7th and Jackson.

CITY OFFICERS.

City council rooms Monroe street between 7th and 8th.

Mayor—JOHN McCREERY.
City Clerk—H. C. WATSON.
Treasurer—PRESCO WRIGHT.
Supervisor—JOHN NELCH.
Marshal—WM. MALONEY.

City Attorney—THOS. SRERLING.
Comptroller—J. H. McDONALD.
Engineer—JOSEPH LEDLIE.
Sexton Oak Ridge—W. F. BICKES.
Prison Keeper—JACOB ALYEA.

ALDERMEN.

First Ward.

ANTONIO VIEIRA.
JOHN FOSTER.
FRANK JACOBY.

Second Ward.

JAS. WILLIAMS.
GEO. RITTER.
JOHN. FITZGERALD.

Third Ward.

HENRY GRUBB.
JAS. W. SMITH.
JOSEPH WALLACE.

Fourth Ward.

BARTLEY CONLON.
RICHARD O'DONNELL.
GEO. KERN.

Fifth Ward.

E. S. JOHNSON.
JOHN O. RAMES.

Sixth Ward.

JOHN T. RHODES.
H. FAYART.
WM. DRAKE.

BOARD OF SUPERVISORS OF SANGAMON COUNTY.

ABLE, JAS. A., *Auburn.*
BRADEEN, A. R., *Springfield.*
CARPENTER, GEO., *Capital.*
CARTER, P. S., *Loami.*
CONCKLING, C. L., *Capital.*
CONNELLY, W. C., *Capital.*
CRABB, J. D., *Woodside.*
DAVIS, H. R., *Pawnee.*
DODD, J. E., *Talkington.*
FAY, BRYANT, *Island Grove.*
FINNEY, WM., *Rochester.*
FLAGG, CORNELIUS, *Fancy Creek.*
FREY, ANTON, *Curran,*
GODLEY, FRANK, *Capital.*
GRUBB, SAM. A., *Clear Lake.*
HALL, OLIVER P., *Mechanicsburg.*

HANRATTY, OWEN, *Capital.*
HARNSBERGER, G. L., *Curtwright.*
HERNDON, WM. F., *Capital.*
IRWIN, W. F., *Salisbury.*
KENNEDY, JAS. A., *Springfield.*
MATTHEW, S. T., *Ball.*
MUNCE, THOS., *Wheatfield.*
PEDEN, D. W., *Illiopolis.*
PRIEST, J. W., *Capital.*
ROBINSON, WM. B., *Buffalo Hart.*
SPENGLER, HARTMAN, *Cotton Hill.*
TALBOTT, BEN. F., *Capital.*
THAYER, E. R., *Chatham.*
TURNER, NOAH, *Gardner.*
WARREN, WM. M., *New Berlin.*
WEBSTER, O. S., *Williams.*

WIGGINTON, JOHN W., *Cooper.*

SOCIETIES.

MASONIC.

L. L. Munn, Freeport, Ill., Gr. Sec. A. F. & A. M.

Masonic Hall on Monroe street opposite Post Office.

Springfield Lodge, No. 4, Meets first Monday in each month.

Central Lodge, No. 71, Meets second Monday in each month.

Tyrian Lodge, No. 333, Meets third Monday in each month.

St. Paul's Lodge, No. 500, Meets second Tuesday in each month.

Springfield Chapter, No. 1, Meets fourth Monday in each month.

Elwood Commandery, No. 6. *K. T.*, Meets first Thursday in each Month.

KNIGHTS OF U. B. OF THE W.

Esperanza Commandery No. 8, *of Ills.*, Meets every first and third Tuesday evenings in the month, in the Opera House Block, George McCutcheon, Commander; Wm. L. Gardner, Chief of Records.

A. O. U. W.

Sir Knights:—*Constantine Legion No.* 1, *of Ill.*, Meets every second and fourth Tuesday evenings in the month, in Opera House Block. B. F. Spangler, Commander; Wm. L. Gardner, Recorder.

THE FOLLOWING MEET OVER CITY LIBRARY.

Springfield Lodge, No. 37, Meets every Wednesday evening. T. W. Shutt, M. W.; J. D. Roper, Recorder.

Capital City Lodge, No. 38, Meets every Thursday evening. S. H. Gehlman, M. W.; J. L. Holtman, Recorder.

Good Will Lodge, No. 39, Meets every Saturday evening. W. Bartram, M. W.; F. E. Earley, Recorder.

Mozart (German) Lodge, No. 106, Meets every Monday evening. Sam'l Rubly, M. W.; Hy. Brand, Recorder.

WORKMEN'S BUILDING AND LOAN ASSOCIATION.

Meets every second Thursday in month in Opera House Block. J. M. Rippey, President; Wm. L. Gardner, Secretary.

ODD FELLOWS.

Sangamon Lodge, No. 6, meets every Wednesday evening, over State National Bank. W. A. Young, N. G.; Antonio Frank, V. G.; T. A. Withey, R. S.; Henry Engelskirchen, P. S.; H. O. Bolles, Treasurer.

Tutonia Lodge, No. 166, meets every Wednesday evening, over State National Bank. William Helmle, N. G.; Jacob Felber, V. G.; Emil Fritsch, Secretary; J. M. Striffler, Treasurer.

Prairie State Encampment, No. 16, meets on the first and third Mondays of every month, over State National Bank. David Simpson, C. P.; W. M. Duggans, H. P.; E. P. Beach, S. W.; W. H. Davis, J. W.

Schiller Encampment, No. 121, meets every first and third Friday in the month, over State National Bank. Rudolph Hellweg, C. P.; Charles Fehr, H. P.; Fred. Weiss, S. W.; George Ritter, Scribe and Treasurer.

Springfield Lodge, No. 465, meets every Thursday evening, over State National Bank. A. Orendorff, N. G.; J. O. Rames, V. G.; John C. Hughes, R. S.; John W. Withey, P. S.; O. F. Stebbins, Treasurer; J. O. Humphrey, S. P. G.

KNIGHTS OF PYTHIAS.

Capitol Lodge, No. 14, meets every Monday evening, in Library Building. J. P. Lindley, P. C.; C. G. Averill, C. C.; B. F. Talbott, V. C.; S. J. Willett, Prelate; J. H. Freeman, M. of E.; R. A. Higgins, M. of F.; J. D. Roper, K. of R. S.; T. E. Shutt, M. at A.; J. W. Young, I. G.; J. B. Kuecher, O. G.

TYPOGRAPHICAL UNION.

Springfield Typographical Union have elected the following officers for the ensuing year: John E. Allen, President; A. M. Barkor, Vice-President; H. T. Schlick, Financial Secretary; Howard Williams, Recording Secretary; Timothy Collins, Treasurer; Louis J. Bender, Sergeant-at-Arms; John Ankrom, P. J. Doyle, Charles Bradley. Thomas Thorpe, Arthur S. Hoag, Executive Committee.

BENEFICIARY ASSOCIATIONS.

German-American Savings and Loan Association, of Springfield, Illinois, incorporated July, 1879. Monthly payments fifty cents per share of $100 each. Frank Reisch, President; Alfred Oren-torff, Vice-President; O. F. Stebbins, Treasurer; Charles Herman, Secretary.

Workingmen's Savings and Homestead Association, of Springfield, Illinois, incorporated in 1872. Weekly payments of twenty-five cents per share of $100 each. Frank Hudson, Jr., President; George Ritter, Vice-President; Albert Stiger, Treasurer; Jacob Ritter, Secretary.

Young Men's Christian Association, opposite post-office. W. F. Bischoff, Secretary.

Springfield Library Association, corner Fifth and Monroe. Mrs. Hanna M. Kimball, Librarian.

Springfield Turn Verein, meets every second Thursday, over Kreigh's store, south Fifth street. G. Wendlandt, President; G. Jones, Treasurer; Henry Schlange, Secretary.

HEBREW SOCIETIES.

Emes Lodge No. 67, I. O. B. B., meets in rear of Temple, up stairs, every first and third Sunday of each month. B. A. Lange, President; Z. Levy, Vice-President; D. Seligman, Secretary; S. Hess, Treasurer. This lodge belongs to District No. 6; has a relief fund of $2,400, and pays $5 a week to sick brethren.

Berith Sholem Congregation, owns a beautiful temple on North 5th, near State Arsenal, and meets every Friday evening for service. S. Benjamin, President; S. Rosenwald, Vice-President; S. Hammerslough, Secretary; B. A. Lange, Treasurer.

Ladies' Benevolent Society, meets first Wednesday in January, April, July and October, in Sunday School room, and pays weekly sick benefits of $3. Mrs. S. Hammerslough, President; Mrs. H. Stern, Vice-President; Mrs. C. Seaman, Secretary; Mrs. S. Benjamin, Treasurer.

CHURCHES.

BAPTIST.

CENTRAL.—Corner 4th and Capitol Avenue.
Rev. F. D. RICKERSON, Pastor.

GERMAN.—Capitol Avenue, bet. 5th and 6th.
Rev. WM. PAPENHAUSEN, Pastor.

UNION.—(Colored) Corner 12th and Mason.
Rev. ROBERTSON, Pastor.

ZION.—(Colored) Corner 9th and Carpenter.
Rev. GEORGE BRENTS, Pastor.

CHRISTIAN.

Corner 5th and Jackson.　　　Rev. J. B. ALLEN, Pastor.

CONGREGATIONAL.

Corner 5th and Edwards.　　　Rev. R. O. POST, Pastor.

CATHOLIC.

IMMACULATE CONCEPTION.—Corner 7th and Monroe.
Rev. P. BRADY, Pastor.
Rev. P. BOURKE, Assistant Pastor.

ST. JOSEPH'S.—N. 6th, near Convent. Rev. M. KANE, Pastor.

SS. PETER AND PAUL.—Corner 6th and Reynolds.
Rev. F. G. LEVE, Pastor.

EPISCOPAL.

ST. PAUL'S.—Corner 3d and Adams.
Rev. E. A. LARRABEE, Rector.

HEBREW TEMPLE.

North 5th, near State Arsenal. Rev. CHAS. AUSTRIAN, Pastor,

LUTHERAN.

ENGLISH.—Corner 6th and Madison.
Rev. B. F. CROUSE, Pastor.

TRINITY.—South 3d, near Washington.
Rev. F. LOCHNER, Pastor.

ST. JOHN'S.—Corner 3d and Washington.
Rev. L. W. GRAEFF, Pastor.

CHURCHES—Continued.

METHODIST.

First.—Corner 5th and Monroe. Rev. T. A. Parker, Pastor.

Second.—North 5th, bet. Madison and Mason.
Rev. S. W. Matthews, Pastor.

German.—Corner 7th and Mason.
Rev. J. H. Miller, Pastor.

St. Paul's.—(Colored) 4th and Mason.
Rev. J. Dawson, Pastor.

PRESBYTERIAN.

First.—Corner 7th and Capitol Avenue.
Rev. J. A. Reed, Pastor.

Second.—Corner 4th and Monroe.
Rev. David S. Johnson, Pastor.

Third.—Corner 6th and North Grand Avenue.
Rev. E. S. McMichael, Pastor.

First Portuguese.—Madison, bet. 4th and 5th.
Rev. A. Liet, Pastor.

Second Portuguese.—Corner 8th and Miller.
Rev. Manuel Piers, Pastor.

U. S. OFFICERS.

Postmaster—Paul Selby.
Collector—Jonathan Merriam.
U. S. Marshal—Jacob Wheeler.

STATE OFFICERS.

Governor—SHELBY M. CULLOM; $6,000.
Lieut. Governor—JOHN M. HAMILTON; $1,000.
Secretary—HENRY D. DEMENT; $3,500.
Auditor—CHARLES P. SWIGERT; $3,500.
Treasurer—EDWARD RUTZ; $3,500.
Att'y-General—JAMES McCARTNEY; $3,500.
Sup't Pub. Inst.—JAMES P. SLADE; $3,500.
Adj't General—ISAAC H. ELLIOTT; $2,000.

STATE BOARDS.

Illinois State Board of Public Charities—F. H. WINES, Secretary.

Railroad and Warehouse Commissioners—JOHN MOSES, Secretary.

State Board of Agriculture—S. D. FISHER, Secretary.

State Bureau of Labor Statistics—F.H.B. McDOWELL, Secretary.

State Board of Health—JOHN H. RAUCH, Secretary.

State Historical Library—A. H. WORTHEN, Curator.

State Board of Pharmacy—Herman Schroeder, Adams Co.; Chas. W. Day, Wabash Co.; John E. Espy, McLean Co.; Frank Fleury, Sangamon Co.; Geo. Buck, Cook Co.;

State Board of Dental Examiners—Green V. Black, Morgan Co.; George H. Cushing and A. W. Harlan, Cook Co.; J. J. Jennelle, Perry Co.; O. Wilson, Kane Co.

Public Administrators –George W. Martin, Cass Co.; George B. Crooker, Christian Co.; Robert C. Maxwell, Logan Co.; Jerome R. Gorin, Macon Co.; Walter A. Clinch, Peoria Co.; R. H. Mann, Randolph Co., Russell H. Curtis, Rock Island Co.; William J. Conkling, Sangamon Co.; Henry M. Needles, St. Clair Co.; A. J. Matson, Whiteside Co. Holding office four years.

Signal Corps—A. T. B. JENNINGS, Observer in charge, Post-office.

Branch Census Office, 521 Monroe—FRED. H .WINES, Special agt.

GOVERNMENT OFFICERS.

President—C. A. ARTHUR.
Vice-President—DAVID DAVIS.
Secretary of State—JAMES G. BLAINE.
Secretary of Treasury—WILLIAM WINDOM.
Secretary of War—ROBERT T. LINCOLN.
Secretary of Navy—WILLIAM H. HUNT.
Secretary of Interior—SAMUEL J. KIRKWOOD.
Postmaster General—THOMAS L. JAMES.
Attorney General—WAYNE MacVEIGH.

The President's salary being $50,000; Vice-President's, $8,000; members of the Cabinet each, $8,000.

OFFICERS U. S. COURTS

Circuit Judge—THOMAS DRUMMOND.

District Judge—SAMUEL H. TREAT.

District Attorney—JAMES A. CONNOLLY.

Assistant District attorney— EDWARD T. ROE.

Clerk Circuit Court—JOHN A. JONES.

Clerk District Court—M. B. CONVERSE.

Register in Bankruptcy—N. W. BRANSON and M. B. CONVERSE.

U. S. Commissioners—L. B. ADAMS and M. B. CONVERSE.

COURTS.

Supreme Court meets the first Tuesdays in June and January.

Appellate Court meets the 3d Tuesdays in May and November.

Circuit Court meets the first Mondays in February, May and October. Judge Zane, presiding.

County Court meets the second Mondays in April, July and December. Judge Matheny, presiding.

United States Court meets the 1st Mondays in June and January.

RAILROADS.

Chicago, Alton & St. Louis R. R.—Depot corner 3d and Jefferson. J. C. McMullin, general sup't.; James Charlton, general passenger agent: J. P. Lindley, local ticket agent.

Ohio & Mississippi R. R.—Depot corner 5th and Madison; C. M. Stanton, division sup't.

Illinois Central.—Depot corner 5th and Madison; W. Wilkinson, division sup't.; James E. Hudson, freight agent.

Wabash, St. Louis & Pacific R. R.—Depot corner 10th and Washington; Robert Andrews, general sup't., Toledo, O.; H. F. Clark, division sup't., Springfield; H. C. Townsend, general passenger agent, St. Louis; Theo. McEuen, local ticket agent.

Springfield & Northwestern R. R.—Depot corner 10th and Washington. E. B. Hyde, sup't.; Fred. W Sutton, auditor.

NEWSPAPERS.

ILLINOIS STATE JOURNAL (daily and weekly), 315 S 6th. Springfield Journal Co., publishers,

ILLINOIS STATE REGISTER (daily and weekly), 514 Monroe. Smith, Clendenin & Rees, publishers.

ILLINOIS FREIE PRESSE (weekly), 415 Jefferson. Fred. Gehring, publisher.

MORNING MONITOR (daily and weekly), 615 Monroe. T. W. S. Kidd, publisher.

STAATS-WOCHENBLATT (weekly), 513 East Monroe. Henry Schlange, publisher.

EVENING POST, (daily), northwest cor. 6th and Monroe, Springer's building. F. H. P. McDowell, publisher.

PUBLISHING, BINDING AND STEREOTYPING. H. W. Rokker, 309 South 5th St.

BLANK BOOK MANUFACTORY. H. W. Rokker, 309 South 5th St.

EXPRESS COMPANIES.

American Express Co., 322 South 5th; M. G. Hall, agent.

U. S. and Pacific Express Cos., 203 South 5th; J. W. Carter, agent.

TELEGRAPH AND TELEPHONE.

Western Union Telegraph Co., northwest corner 6th and Monroe; W. W. Kelchner, manager.

Mutual Union Telegraph Co., 212 South 6th St., Central Block.

Central Telephone Co., over 214 South 5th.

CENSUS OF THE CITY OF SPRINGIELD.

October 1st, 1881...................................22,155

CENSUS OF THE UNITED STATES, 1880.

Males....................................... 25,520,582
Females..................................... 24,632,284

Total....................................... 50,152,866

The following is a list of the State officers since the formation of the State government of Illinois to the present time:

GOVERNORS.

Shadrach Bond, St. Clair county, inaugurated	Oct.	6, 1818.
Edward Coles, Madison county,	"	Dec.	5, 1822.
Ninian Edwards, Madison county,	"	Dec.	6, 1826.
John Reynolds, St. Clair county,	"	Dec.	9, 1830.
Wm. L. D. Ewing, Fayette county,	"	Nov.	17, 1834.
Joseph Duncan, Morgan county,	"	Dec.	3, 1834.
Thomas Carlin, Greene county,	"	Dec.	7, 1838.
Thomas Ford, Ogle county,	"	Dec.	8, 1842.
Augustus C. French, Crawford county,	"	Dec.	9, 1846.
Augustus C. French, Crawford county,	"	Jan.	8, 1849.
Joel A. Matteson, Will county,	"	Jan.	—, 1853.
Wm. H. Bissell, Monroe county,	"	Jan.	12, 1857.
John Wood, Adams county,	"	Mar.	21, 1860.
Richard Yates, Morgan county,	"	Jan.	14, 1861.
Richard J. Oglesby, Macon county,	"	Jan.	16, 1865.
John M. Palmer, Macoupin county,	"	Jan.	11, 1869.
Richard J. Oglesby, Macon county,	"	Jan.	13, 1873.
John L. Beveridge, Cook county,	"	Jan.	23, 1873.
Shelby M. Cullom, Sangamon county,	"	Jan.	8, 1877.
Shelby M. Cullom, Sangamon county,	"	Jan.	10, 1881.

LIEUTENANT-GOVERNORS.

Pierre Menard, Randolph county, inaugurated	Oct.	6, 1818.
Adolphus F. Hubbard, Galatin county,	"	Dec.	5, 1822.
William Kinney, St. Clair county,	"	Dec.	6, 1826.
Zadoc Casey, Jefferson county,	"	Dec.	9, 1830.
Wm. L. D. Ewing, Fayette county,	"	Mar.	1, 1833.
Alex. M. Jenkins, Jackson county,	"	Dec.	5, 1834.
Wm. H. Davidson, White county,	"	Dec.	6, 1836.
Stinson H. Anderson, Jefferson county,	"	Dec.	7, 1838.
John Moore, McLean county,	"	Dec.	8, 1842.
Joseph B. Wells, Rock Island county,	"	Dec.	9, 1846.
Wm. McMurtry, Knox county,	"	Jan.	8, 1849.
Gustavus Koerner, St. Clair county,	"	Jan.	—, 1853.
John Wood, Adams county,	"	Jan.	12, 1857.
Thomas A. Marshall, Coles county,	"	Jan.	7, 1861.
Francis A. Hoffman, Cook county,	"	Jan.	14, 1861.
William Bross, Cook county,	"	Jan.	16, 1865.
John Dougherty, Union county,	"	Jan.	11, 1869.
John L. Beveridge, Cook county,	"	Jan.	13, 1873.
John Early, Winnebago county,	"	Jan.	23, 1873.
Archibald A. Glenn, Brown county,	"	Jan.	8, 1875.
Andrew Shuman, Cook county,	"	Jan.	8, 1877.
John M. Hamilton, McLean county,	"	Jan.	10, 1881.

SECRETARIES OF STATE.

Elias Kent Kane, Kaskaskia county, qualified,	Oct.	6, 1818.
Sam'l D. Lockwood, Madison county, "	Dec.	18, 1822.
David Blackwell, St. Clair county, "	April	2, 1823.
Morris Birkbeck, Edwards county, "	Oct.	15, 1824.
George Forquer, Sangamon county, "	Jan.	17, 1825.
Alexander P. Field, Union county, "	Dec.	31, 1828.
Stephen A. Douglas, Morgan county, "	Nov.	30, 1840.
Lyman Trumbull, St. Clair county, "	Feb.	27, 1841.
Thompson Campbell, JoDaviess county, "	Mar.	4, 1843.
Horace S. Cooley, Adams county, "	Dec.	23, 1846.
Horace S. Cooley, Adams county, "	Jan.	8, 1849.
David L. Gregg, Cook county, "	Apr.	10, 1850.
Alexander Starne, Pike county, "	Jan.	10, 1853.
Ozias M. Hatch, Pike county, "	Jan.	12, 1857.
Ozias M. Hatch, Pike county, "	Jan.	14, 1861.
Sharon Tyndale, St. Clair county, "	Jan.	16, 1865.
Edward Rummel, Peoria county, "	Jan.	11, 1869.
George H. Harlow, Tazewell county, "	Jan.	13, 1873.
George H. Harlow, Tazewell county, "	Jan.	8, 1877.
Henry D. Dement, Lee county "	Jan.	10, 1881.

STATE TREASURERS.

John Thomas, St. Clair county......qualified,	........1818.
R. K. McLaughlin, Fayette county, "	Aug. 2, 1819.
Abner Field, Union county, "	Jan. 14, 1823.
James Hall, Jackson county, "	Feb. 12, 1827.
John Dement, Franklin county, "	Feb. 5, 1831.
Charles Gregory, Greene county, "	Dec. 5, 1836.
John D. Whiteside, Monroe county, "	Mar. 4, 1837.
Milton Carpenter, Hamilton county, "	Mar. 6, 1841.
John Moore, McLean county, "	Aug. 14, 1848.
John Moore, McLean county, "	Dec. 16, 1850.
James Miller, McLean county, "	Jan. 12, 1857.
William Butler, Sangamon county, "	Sep. 3, 1859.
William Butler, Sangamon county, "	Jan. 14, 1861.
Alexander Starne, Sangamon county, "	Jan. 12, 1863.
James H. Beveridge, DeKalb county, "	Jan. 9, 1865.
George W. Smith, Cook county, "	Jan. 10, 1867.
Erastus N. Bates, Marion county, "	Jan. 11, 1869.
Erastus N. Bates, Marion county, "	Nov. 8, 1870.
Edward Rutz, St. Clair county, "	Jan. 13, 1873.
Thos. S. Ridgeway, Gallatin county, "	Jan. 11, 1875.
Edward Rutz, St. Clair county, "	Jan. 8, 1877.
John C. Smith, Jo Daviess county, "	Jan. 13, 1879.
Edward Rutz, Cook county, "	Jan. 10, 1881.

AUDITOR PUBLIC ACCOUNTS.

Elijah C. Berry, Fayette county,	qualified,	Oct.	9,	1818.
Elijah C. Berry, Fayette county.	"	Apr.	6,	1819.
James T. B. Stapp, Fayette county,	"	Aug.	27,	1831.
Levi Davis, Fayette county,	"	Nov.	16,	1835.
James Shields, Randolph county,	"	Mar.	4,	1841.
Wm. L. D. Ewing, Fayette county,	"	Mar.	26,	1843.
Thos. H. Campbell, Randolph county,	"	Mar.	26,	1836.
Thos. H. Campbell, Randolph county,	"	Jan.	7,	1847.
Jesse K. Dubois, Lawrence county,	"	Jan.	12,	1857.
Jesse K. Dubois, Lawrence county,	"	Jan.	14,	1861.
Orlin H. Miner, Sangamon county,	"	Dec.	12,	1864.
Charles E. Lippincott, Cass county,	"	Jan.	11,	1869.
Charles E. Lippincott, Cass county,	"	Jan.	13,	1873.
Thos. B. Needles, Washington county,	"	Jan.	8,	1877.
Chas. P. Swigert, Kankakee county,	"	Jan.	10,	1881.

ATTORNEYS GENERAL.

Daniel Pope Cook, Randolph county,	qualified,	Mar.	3,	1819.
William Mears, St. Clair county,	"	Dec.	14,	1819.
Sam'l D. Lockwood, Madison county,	"	Feb.	26,	1821.
James Turney, Washington county,	"	Jan.	14,	1823.
James Turney, Washington county,	"	Jan.	15,	1825.
George Forquer, Monroe county,	"	Jan.	23,	1829.
James Semple, Madison county,	"	Jan.	30,	1833.
Ninian W. Edwards, Sangamon county,	"	Sep.	1,	1834.
Ninian W. Edwards, Sangamon county,	"	Jan.	19,	1835.
Jesse B. Thomas, Jr., Madison county,	"	Feb.	12,	1835.
Walter B. Scates, Jefferson county,	"	Jan.	18,	1836.
Usher F. Linder, Coles county	"	Feb.	4,	1837.
George W. Olney, Madison county,	"	June	26,	1838.
Wickliffe Kitchell, Crawford county,	"	Mar.	5,	1839.
Josiah Lamborn, Morgan county,	"	Dec.	23,	1840.
James A. McDougall, Morgan county,	"	Jan.	12,	1843.
David B. Campbell, Sangamon county,	"	Dec.	21,	1846.
Robert G. Ingersoll, Peoria county,	"	Feb.	28,	1867.
Washington Bushnell, LaSalle county,	"	Jan.	11,	1869.
James K. Edsall, Lee county,	"	Jan.	13,	1873.
James K. Edsall, Lee county,	"	Jan.	8,	1877.
James McCartney, Wayne county,	"	Jan.	10,	1881.

STATE ENTOMOLOGISTS.

D. B. Walsh, Rock Island county,	appointed,	June	11,	1867.
William LeBarron, Kane county,	"	April	2,	1870.
Cyrus Thomas, Jackson county,	"	April	13,	1875.

SUPERINTENDENTS PUBLIC INSTRUCTION.

Ninian W. Edwards, Sangamon co'ty, qualified Mar. 24, 1854.
William H. Powell, Peoria county, " Jan. 12, 1857.
Newton Bateman, Morgan county, " Jan. 1, 1859.
Newton Bateman, Morgan county, " Jan. 4, 1861.
John P. Brooks, Sangamon county, " Jan. 12, 1863.
Newton Bateman, Sangamon county, " Jan. 10, 1865.
Newton Bateman, Sangamon county, " Jan. —, 1867.
Newton Bateman, Sangamon county, " Jan. —, 1871.
Samuel M. Etter, McLean county, " Jan. 11, 1875.
James P. Slade, St. Clair county, " Jan. 13, 1879.

STATE GEOLOGISTS.

Jos. G. Norwood, Sangamon county, appointed, July 21, 1851.
H. A. Ulffers, Hardin county, " ———, 1853.
Amos H. Worthen, Hancock county, " Mar. 22, 1858.
Leopold Richter, St. Louis, Mo., " Dec. 1, 1859.
Henry Engelmann, St. Clair county, " Apr. 19, 1861.
William Billington, Sangamon county, " Apr. 26, 1864.

ADJUTANTS GENERAL.

Wm. Alexander, Randolph county, appointed April 24, 1819.
Elijah C. Berry, Fayette county, " June 11, 1821.
James W. Berry, Fayette county. " Dec. 19, 1828.
Moses K. Anderson, Sangamon county, " Dec. 16, 1839.
Simon B. Buckner, Cook county, " April 3, 1857.
William C. Kinney, St. Clair county, " Dec. 9, 1857.
Thos. S. Mather, Sangomon county, " Oct. 28, 1858.
Allen C. Fuller, Boone county, " Nov. 11, 1861.
Isham N. Haynie. Alexander county, " Jan. 16, 1865.
Edward P. Niles, Cook county, " . . . .
Hubert Dilger, Sangamon county, " Mar. 24, 1869.
Edwin L. Higgins, Sangamon county, " Jan. 24, 1873.
Edwin L. Higgins, Sangamon county, " July 1, 1874.
Hiram Hilliard, Cook county, " July 2, 1875.
Hiram Hilliard, Cook county, " July 2, 1877.

SPRINGFIELD WATER WORKS.

LOCATION OF FIRE PLUGS.

Single.. . .S. W. corner of 9th and Carpenter.
Single.... .N. W. corner of 9th and Mason.
Single.... .N. W. corner of 9th and Jefferson.
Double....S. W. corner of 9th and Monroe.
Single.... .N. E. corner of 9th and Jackson.
Double....N. W. corner of 9th and Cook.
Double....S. W. corner of 8th and Cook.
Double ...S. W. corner of 7th and Enos Avenue.
Double. ..S. E. corner of 7th and Carpenter.
Double....N. W. corner of 7th and Carpenter.
Single.... .S. E. corner of 7th and Mason.
Double ...N. W. corner of 7th and Jefferson.
Double....N. W. corner of 7th and Washington.
Double....S. W. corner of 7th and Adams.
Double....S. W. corner of 7th and Monroe.
Double....Sixth Ward Engine House.
Single.... .S. W. corner of 7th and Jackson.
Double....N. E. corner of 7th and Cook.
Double....N. W. corner of 7th and Allen.
Single.... .N. E. corner of 6th and Adams.
Single.... .S. W. corner of 6th and Adams.
Single. ...N. W. corner 6th and Alley bet. Monroe and Cap. Av.
Single   .N. W. corner of Leland Hotel.
Single.... .S. W. corner of 6th and Capitol Avenue.
Single.... .N. E. corner of 6th and Cook.
Single.... .N. E. corner of 6th and Cass.
Double....N. E. corner of 6th and Allen.
Double.. .S. E. corner of 5th and Enos Avenue.
Double... N. E. corner of 5th and Carpenter.
Single ....N. E. corner of 5th and Madison.
Single.... .S. W. corner of 5th and Jefferson.
Double....N. E. corner of 5th and Jefferson.
Double....S. W. corner of 5th and Washington.

LOCATION OF FIRE PLUGS—*Continued.*

Double....N. W. corner of 5th and Adams.
Double ...S. E. corner of 5th and Adams.
Double....N. W. corner of 5th and Monroe.
Double....S. E. corner of 5th and Monroe.
Double....S. E. corner of 4th and Monroe.
Single.....S. E. corner of 4th and Jackson.
Single.....S. E. corner of 4th and Cook.
Single.....S. W. corner of 4th and Canady.
Double....N. W. corner of 4th and Allen.
Double....S. W. corner of 2d and Carpenter.
Single.....S. W. corner of 2d and Mason.
Single.....S. W. corner of 2d and Jefferson.
Double....N. E. corner of 2d and Jefferson.
Double....N. E. corner of 2d and Washington.
Double....S. E. corner of 2d and Adams.
Double....S. E. corner of 2d and Monroe.
Double....N. W. corner of 2d and Edwards.
Single.....S. E. corner of 2d and Wright.
Double....N. E. corner of 2d and Allen.
Double....S. W. corner of Spring and Monroe.
Single.....S. W. corner of Pasfield and Monroe.
Double....S. E. corner of Walnut and Monroe.
Double....N. E. corner of Edwards and Walnut.
Double....N. E. corner of Edwards and Spring.
Single.....S. E. corner of 10th and Jefferson.
Single.....S. E. corner of 6th and Jefferson.
Double....S. E. corner of 6th and Washington.
Single.....N. W. corner of 8th and Washington.
Single.....N. E. corner of 6th and Jackson.
Single.....N. E. corner of 7th and Cass.
Single.....S. W. corner of Edwards and Pasfield.
Single.....N. E. corner of Edwards and New.
Single.....S. W. corner of Monroe and New.
Single.....S. E. corner of 2d and Canady.
Single.....N. E. corner of Carpenter and Klein.
Single.....N. E. corner of Carpenter and Rutledge.
Double....Second Ward Engine House.
Single.....N. E. corner of 9th and Adams.
Single.....N. E. corner of Rutledge and Miller.

Location of Fire Plugs—*Continued.*

Double....S. E. corner of Rutledge and Herndon.
Single.....S. E. corner of 11th and Jackson.
Single.....S. E. corner of 11th and Monroe.
Single.....S. E. corner of 11th and Washington.
Single.....S. E. corner of 11th and Mason.
Single.....S. E. corner of 12th and Jefferson.
Single.   S. E. corner of 13th and Mason.
Single.....N. E. corner of 13th and Washington.
Single.....N. E. corner of 13th and Monroe.
Single.....N. E. corner of 13th and Jackson.
Single.....N. E. corner of 14th and Madison.
Single.....East side of 4th bet. Jackson and Market.
Single.....S. E. corner of 6th and Clay.
Single.....North side of Madison bet. 15th and Chestnut.
Single.....N. E. corner of 9th and Enos Avenue.
Single.....N. W. corner of 9th and Lincoln.
Single.....S. E. corner of 9th and Division.
Single.....S. W. corner of 9th and N. Grand Avenue.
Single.....S. E. corner of 11th and N. Grand Avenue.
Single.....N. E. corner of 4th and Mason.

H. O. BOLLES, *President.*

GEO. WITHEY, *Treasurer.*

L. R. BROWN, *Secretary.*

FRED. McCARTHY, *Supt.*

JOHN DOUGHTON, *Tapper.*

WM. McCABE, *Resr. Watchman.*

F. L. WHEATLEY, *Engineer.*

H. O. BOLLES,
GEORGE WITHEY, } *Commissioners.*
OBED LEWIS,

EAST AVENUE.

FIRST WARD.

FOURTH WARD.

Washington Street.

Wabash Railway.   Tenth Street.

NORTH AVENUE.

SOUTH AVENUE.

FIFTH WARD.

SIXTH WARD.

Fifth St.

C., A. & St. Louis Railroad.   Third Street.

Adams Street

SECOND WARD.

THIRD WARD.

Washt'n St

Lewis St.

WEST AVENUE.

KNOX'S

SPRINGFIELD CITY DIRECTORY

FOR 1881-2.

ABBREVIATIONS:

E or e east; W or w west; N or n north; S or s south; av avenue; cor corner; ne northeast; se southeast; nw northwest; sw southwest; bet between; N G north grand; S G south grand; E G east grand; W G west grand; nr near; res resides or residence; es east side; ws west side; ns north side; ss south side.

ABEL R P, 524 S 5th
Ackermann Phillip, 555 W Mason
Adderley Dr Fred, 934 S Spring
Abels Martin, 826 W Washington
Adams Geo, 925 S 12th
Adams Mrs Dr, W Jefferson w of Walnut
Adams Mrs, 820 E Washington, dress making
Adams Henry, 313 W Wright
Adams William, 1309 S 11th
Adams L B, 305 E Madison
Adams Isaac, se cor 10th and Mason, saloon
Ackard Jacob, 1110 S 4th
Affonso M, 1029 E Mason
Aitken Wm F, 936 S 5th
Alderdice Wm, cor 18th and Monroe
Alexander G F, 637 N 2d
Allen Patrick, 1513 E Adams
Allison Mrs J M, S 18th and Kansas
Allen Mrs H A, 211 W Jackson
Allen Patrick, 1308 E Jackson
Allen Mrs Mary, 17th and Capitol av
Allen Mrs Hannah, sw cor 10th and Madison
Allen F, 1631 E Jackson
Allen Wm I, 1203 S 8th
—4

Allen Harrison, 714 S 15th
Allen G W. W Washington w of 1st
Allman John, 1st and Miller
Allen J B, 206 S Walnut
Allen Wm S, 413 N 6th
Allen Joel, nw cor Spring and Scarritt
Allen John E, 914 E Monroe
Allen F, 1631 E Jackson
Allen Robt, 612 S 5th
Allyn N L. 915 S 5th
Allman John jr, W Carpenter w of Cox
Alwood Thos, 1111 N 5th
Alyward Thos, 410 W Adams
Alyea Jacob, city prison kpr res at same
Almida Toney, 123 E Carpenter
Almon Mary, 1024½ E Mason
Ambrose D L, 919 N 6th
American Express Co, 222 S 5th
Ambrose John, cor 15th and Clay
Ammann A, 1113 S 8th
Anderson J L, corn doctor nr Marine Bank
Anderson Mrs, 1402 E Monroe
Anderson John, Adams bet 3d and 4th
Andrews Wm, N 7th bet Carpenter and Miller
Anderson J L. E Monroe bet 9th and 10th
Anderson John, E Monroe bet 9th and 10th
Anderson L S. 121½ ws square, photograph gallery
Anderson John H, 427 W Adams
Anderson Geo W, 1153 N G Ave bet 5th and 6th
Anderson Mrs H C, 1303 E Jackson
Anderson Jas, Cass bet 17th and 18th
Anderson J H, 1518 E Mason
Anderson Geo E, Douglas and Grand av
Anderson F E. Capital Avenue bet 14th and 15th
Anderson M K, nw cor Jefferson and Klein
Anderson G W, 301 W Canedy
Anderson Joseph. 316 W Adams
Anderson L S, N 9th bet Division and N G av
Andrews John, 1029 E Madison
Andrews Geo, W Wright
Anstice E V, N 11th bet Madison and Mason
Anglan Frank, W Jefferson and Mill
Ansell Wm, 105 W Allen
Andrews Mrs Susan. 634 S 5th
Angell Albert E, bet Enos av and Lincoln st
Ankrom Mrs Hulda, 111 S 2d
Anthony Thos, 107 E Carpenter
Armstrong Jas, 1615 E Washington
Armbruster A, 104 E Jefferson

Armstrong Thos, 609 N 4th
Armstrong Mrs J, 526 S 5th
Arnold Erwin, S 9th bet Jackson and Edwards
Artsman Dr E, 810 E Monroe
Arnold A, sw cor Jefferson and John
Arnold Chas, se cor 8th and Jackson
Arnold John, Lincoln bet 11th and 12th
Asburry Robt, se cor Edwards and Spring
Aschauer Chas, 108 W Mason
Asbury Dr I M, 1106 E Jackson
Applett Mrs, 1131 N 5th
Auxier Jefferson, N Klein and Calhoun av
August M, 317 N 14th
Apgar Aaron, 703 N 8th
Averill C G, 913 S 6th
Averitt Thos, 1118 E Jefferson
Averitt N O, N 1st bet Union and Pine
Ayers Byron, 104 W Allen

BAHR JACOB, 1224 S 11th
Baehr Benjamin, S 2d bet Canedy and Scarritt
Bachhelm Conrad, 540 W Mason
Bachhelm, 532 W Mason
Babeuf, 126 (old number) W Capitol av
Babeuf Mrs M, 733 S Spring
Bacon Nelson, se cor 11th and Reynolds
Bailey Jas, 1816 E Washington
Bailey Essie, 116 S 9th
Bailey M B, 413 S 9th
Bailey Mrs L, 509 E Madison
Bailey Mrs S, S 9th bet Washington and Adams
Bailey Pat, 1630 E Capitol av
Bailey Wm, 640 N 3d
Bailey Richard, 309 W Madison
Baker John P, Capitol av bet 7th and 8th
Baker Wm D, N 9th bet Division and N G av
Baker Jas, 209 W Cook
Baker Wm B, 1042 S 4th
Baker Henry, 1204 S 5th
Baker O R, 1234 S 5th
Baker C H, 1017 E Carpenter
Baker Geo, 1117 S 8th
Baker Peter, 321 W Carpenter
Baker Thos, Reservoir bet 11th and 12th
Ball Jacob, se cor 9th and Reynolds
Ball Annie Miss, 1157 N 4th
Ballentine Walter, 223 S 3d
Ballou Geo A, N 6th bet Reynolds and Carpenter
Ballou H W, 1019 E Jefferson

Bancroft Mrs S F, N 1st n of Miller
Bandy E, cor 17th and Edwards
Barlow John, 905 East Mason
Barr John, 1403 E Jackson
Barr B, 723 E Reynolds
Barber R, se cor 11th and Madison
Barber Chas L, 307 W Edwards
Barber Elem, 529 N 11th
Barber W S, 410 W Edwards
Barkley R L, 700 N 6th
Barkley Jas H, 519 S 8th
Barker A M, 728 E Edwards
Bartley M, 1422 E Adams
Bartlet Frank, 1110 N 6th
Barrow John F, 323 S Doyle av
Bartrom Ward, 1169 N 9th
Bartow Wellington, 1101 E Capitol av
Barnard Mrs Annie, 228 E Canedy
Barrington Geo H, 214 S 4th
Barnes Mrs C, sw cor 11th and Miller
Barnes E S, 821 E Cook
Barnes H C, 808 S 5th
Barnes P, 606 S 4th
Barnd Mrs A F, 131 E Carpenter
Barrell Geo, 915 S 4th
Barrett Wm, 830 S Spring
Barry Mrs, 13th bet Douglas and Cass
Barry Jas, 65 (old number) E Edwards
Barry Patrick E, Capitol av bet 9th and 10th
Barry John, 1104 E Mason
Barry John, 713 N 10th
Barry Wm, 826 S 13th
Barry Mrs Pattie, 725 S 2nd
Barron Jas H, W Capitol av
Barron Jas, 1803 E Edwards
Barnatt Thos, 403 West Allen
Bartner Henry, W Washington and John
Bargery M, N Klein bet Jefferson and Madison
Berg F C, 1144 N 5th
Bergold Edward, S 6th bet Vine and S G av
Bartling A, Mason bet 1st and 2nd
Bartling A, cor 18th and Monroe
Boehner Leonard, 229 W Carpenter
Barnauer Geo, sw cor Edwards and Pasfield
Bernauer H, 801 S 15th
Bauman Jacob, S 6th bet Allen and Vine
Bauman V, 912 E Reynolds
Baruldson Erasmus, 13th bet Jackson and Edwards
Baum Joseph, nw cor 4th and Jefferson

Baumgardner Frank, 718 S Spring
Bancom Chas, 322 W Carpenter
Battice A, 321 N 11th
Baxter Andrew, Washington bet 15th and 16th
Beal J R, 531 E Washington (druggist)
Beard Richard, 720 S 12th
Beard R A, 1201 E Cook
Beard Jos, S 4th bet S G av and Vine
Bea Phillip, se cor Rutledge and Calhoun av
Beard Henry, 1507 E Washington
Beach R H, 336 N 5th
Beam Wm C, 224 W Edwards
Beam John C, 603 S Spring
Beardsley Mrs, N 2d bet Washington and Jefferson
Beck John Philip, 912 E Adams
Beecher H H, nw cor 4th and Union
Beck G, 519 N 1st
Bekemeyer Chris, 114 E Cook
Bekemeyer Wm, 413 N 5th
Bell John C, 1126 S 7th
Bell Thos, 1141 N 4th
Bell M E, 1033 N 9th
Bell Mrs, S 15th bet Washington and Adams
Bell John, N 5th bet numbers 428 and 500
Bell D S, 229 W Jackson
Bell Joseph, 13th s of Mason
Belacher John, 1315 S 12th
Bellman Michael, 215 W Reynolds
Bengel John, 715 N 8th
Bengel Fred, 405 N 7th
Bengel Adam, 511 N 6th
Bender John J, 422 W Mason
Bennett Mrs A, S 7th bet Capitol av and Jackson
Bennett Joseph, 511 N 4th
Bennett Joseph, 843 S 5th
Benjamin S, 429 N 6th
Benson N M, 1020 N 5th
Bentz Christian, 909 S Pasfield
Berry Frank, 1103 E Adams
Berry Jacob, 400 W Washington
Berry W C, 215 W Monroe
Berry Jas, 914 E Miller
Berriman Mrs, Mason bet 9th and 10th
Berriman Henry, 225 W Cook
Berriman Peter, S 9th bet Jackson and Edwards
Bergman John, 821 E Miller
Berney Thos, 208 W Cook
Bernard F, 530 N 6th
Bergner M, 1618 E Washington

Bererd Wm, ne cor Mason and 11th
Bergold Theo, 1228 S 7th
Berger Ham, 1130 S 11th
Bied Phillip. 1200 E Capitol ave
Bied Mrs Walter, 731 E Adams
Birnbaum Fred. 343 W Carpenter
Bierbaum John, 1021 E Reynolds
Birnbaum John, se cor 1st and Miller
Bigelow M. 602 S 4th
Billington John, 812 E Carpenter
Billington Wm, sw cor 4th and Union
Billington A M. 1408 E Monroe
Bingham H C, 13th bet Clay and Cass
Bird Sallie, Adams bet 7th and 8th
Birdsong Geo, 1310 E Washington
Birdsong G W, E Washington bet 9th and 10th
Bierce E B, 619 West Capitol av
Bisch Philip, N 6th s of N G av
Bisch Philip, 111 N 6th, furniture
Bishop Thos D, Madison bet 8th and 9th
Bishop Joseph, N 5th bet Mason and Reynolds
Bischoff Chas, N Spring bet Monroe and Adams
Bischoff W F, S 8th bet Edwards and Cook
Bishop Martin, E Brown
Binney Jas, 1116 N 11th
Bittinger J W, 1315 E Capitol av
Biggs Henry, N Doyle av
Black Geo N, 618 S 2d
Black John, S 6th bet Capitol av and Jackson
Blakeman Thos, N 3d bet Carpenter and Union
Blackwell Hester, E Miller and Chesnut
Blume C F, 817 E Madison
Blakesley Frank, 318 N 6th
Bloodgood Samuel, 1165 N 9th
Blumer Wm, 515 N Klein
Bloomer Joseph, 15th bet Washington and Adams
Bloom Chas. S 1st bet Scarritt and Allen
Bobbitt J W, N Doyle av
Bode F, 606 S 7th
Bohmer Mrs L M, E Jefferson bet 4th and 5th
Bogenschuetz, 726 S College
Bohannan Moses, 1225 S 15th
Boehner Geo, 852 N 1st
Burgheim Rev D, 1201 E Jefferson
Boelmer Geo, 128 N 5th, meat market
Boggs Joseph, 812 E Miller
Bogart John, 128 E Adams
Bogardus S, 439 W Edwards
Bolinger John, N 4th bet Carpenter and Union

Bolinger Chas, se cor W Cook and College
Bolinger Geo W, 1014 N 5th
Bolton Mrs, 427 S 12th
Bolte Henry, 117 E Jefferson
Bolin Dan, S 11th s of Douglas
Bolden Jas, cor 14th and Douglas
Boland Mrs, Washington e of 16th
Boney F M, 1130 S 7th
Boon Mrs T B, 833 S 4th
Boon Milton, N 9th bet Madison and Mason
Boon Mrs Eunice, 327 W Calhoun av
Booth Sallie, 1107 E Capitol av
Booth Mrs E, 230 ne cor 9th and Monroe
Booth A S, 500 S 6th
Boothroyd W H, 1014 S Spring
Bostic Joseph, sw cor Mason and Rutledge
Boss Fred, 1133 N 3d
Broeker Edward, 1111 S 11th
Bogue Thos, Reservoir bet 11th and 12th
Bowers Mrs H, 303 E Monroe
Bowen Mrs Geo P, ne cor Monroe and College
Bowerman David, 1109 E Monroe
Bowerman A, 15th n of Madison
Bowe Pat, 1133 E Reservoir
Boyce Wm, W Carpenter w of 441
Bouldnott J, W Washington and State
Boudenot Thos, 1220 S 4th
Bourne Wm H, 323 S 4th
Boyd Mrs E, S 7th bet Capitol av and Jackson
Boyle Micheal, W G av south end
Boyer A, 122 W Carpenter
Bradford John S, S Walnut and Edwards
Bradford Miss Bell, 1106 S 4th
Bradish Walter, S 4th bet Canedy and Wright
Bradsbury Dr, West Mason
Bradley John, cor 10th and Adams
Bradley Mrs Sarah, 612 N 4th
Bradley L H, 413 S 7th
Brandon Dr H, 416 N 5th
Brandt D F, S 8th bet Scarritt and Allen
Brand Wm, W Calhoun av west end
Brand Chas, S 11th bet Jackson and Edwards
Brand Henry, N 4th bet Carpenter and Union
Brand Fred, 623 N 4th
Braxton Jas, 1st bet Washington and Adams
Brantner John D, cor 15th and Douglas
Brassel Dennis, cor 10th and Miller
Bragg H T, 529 N 11th
Brantner Mrs, N 6th bet Reynolds and Carpenter

Brand A, 1216 E Washington
Button J M, 512 S 7th
Britt Mrs Martha H, 908 S on W G av
Bruner Jacob, 905 E Monroe
Bruce Jas, 1429 E Cook
Brennan Thos, 1031 E Washington
Brennan Mrs, cor 7th and Douglas
Brennan Michael S, Doyle av s of Monroe
Brennan John, W Carpenter w of Cox
Brennan Chris, 106 W Jefferson
Brennan Mrs B, 1213 E Madison
Brennan Michael, 726 E Carpenter
Brennan Thos, 6th and Carpenter
Brennan Mrs Margaret, 207 W Mason
Brennan Mrs P, 720 E Carpenter
Brents Rev Geo, 1417 E Adams
Bressmer John, 1105 S 6th
Bressmer Chas, se cor 8th and Cook
Bretz John F, Madison bet 8th and 9th
Breusing Mrs Mary, 807 E Reynolds
Brewer A, 102 W Reynolds
Brewer Jas, W Mason bet 1st and Klein
Brewer Mrs S, 707 E Jefferson
Brewer Mrs M A, Jefferson bet 5th and 6th
Brewer Jas, 913 E Adams
Brewer E, Edwards bet 8th and 9th
Brewer J H, 1118 S 6th
Brewer D F, 615 W Edwards
Bridges Geo H, 841 S 3d
Brinkerhoff John, 816 N 5th
Broadwell N M, 537 S 4th
Broeker Wm, 926 S 7th
Brockel John, 508 W Hay
Broderick, cor 11th and Jackson
Brooks Martin, 12.0 E Jackson
Brooks A M, 515 N 7th
Brooks Rev J F, 617 S 5th
Brooks Geo D, 1015 S 8th
Broderick M, 1129 E Adams
Broderick Patrick, 1036 S Spring
Brown Jas, 527 S Walnut
Brown W H, 729 E Reynolds
Brown L R, 508 S 8th
Brown Daniel, 115 S 2d
Brown Rev Henry, 300 N 10th
Brownie Jessie, 729 E Jefferson
Brown Maggie, 122 N 8th
Brown Patrick, 321 W Reynolds
Brown Mrs B, 919 E Mason

Brown W W, 121 W Jefferson
Brown Wm, 716 E Jefferson
Brown W H, cor 8th and Lincoln
Brown Miss E, 404 S 11th
Brown Albert, 1121 N 7th
Brown Thos M, 1023 N 6th
Brown Wm, S G av bet 10th and 11th
Brown Squire, cor 18th and Cass
Brown Edward, 423 E Washington
Bronson E F, 1426 E Monroe
Bruce Manning A, 228 N 7th
Bruce Harvey, 810 E Miller
Brueck John, 425 N 4th
Brundage C, W Edwards bet Walnut and New
Butze A, 808 E Mason
Bryce Jas P, 214 Doyle av
Bruns H E, cor William and Henrietta
Burchett Henry, 411 S Walnut
Buck Geo, 1031 E Monroe
Buck J R, 1232 S 4th
Buck Dr H B, 712 S 4th
Buck Fred, 406 S 7th
Buckley S, 1104 E Madison
Buckley J T, 923 S Spring
Buchne Wm, 442 W Williams
Bunn Jacob, 435 S 6th
Bondel Mrs, 328 W Miller
Bunker J, 621 W Capitol av
Burch B F, 906 E Carpenter
Burgess Mrs M, cor Cook and Spring
Burk John, 1304 E Jackson
Burt Joseph, S College bet Scarritt and Allen
Burton Harden, 619 E Miller
Burgy Mrs C, 1220 S 7th
Burkhardt G, 716 E Reynolds
Burgess Mrs A, 117 N 4th, up stairs
Burke J B, 417 S 9th
Burfitt Norris, 15th bet Jefferson and Madison
Burton Wm, 15th bet Madison and Mason
Burlingham E P, 411 S 8th
Burns Jas, 12th bet Douglas and Cass
Burns Mrs C, 230 N 13th
Burns M, W Mason bet 1st and Klein
Burns John, Reynolds bet 7th and 8th
Burns F P, 646 N 2d
Burns Mrs, 416 E Jackson
Burns Alexander, 601 W Mason
Burns Michael, 1704 E Cook
—5

Burrill John F, sw cor 6th & Monroe, sec A F & A M
Burrill John F, 1027 S 5th
Busher John & Co, 622 E Adams
Bussing J H, Madison bet 3d and 4th
Burger X, 333 W Mason
Bushard A S, 630 S 11th
Butler Stillman, 18th near Kansas
Butler Miss S, 6th bet Edwards and Cook
Butler Jas, 905 S College
Butler Geo, 911 S College
Butler Mrs, 405 E Monroe
Butler Samuel, nw cor 1st and Jefferson
Butrum J S, N 2d bet Carpenter and Union
Byers Mrs E, 645 N 2d
Byers Chas, 203 S Doyle av
Byerline J G, 114 W Madison
Byerline Casper. 215 W Carpenter
Bryant Mrs E, Capitol av bet 13th and 14th
Bryan John, Madison bet 10th and 11th

CADDIGAN PAT, 1205 S 12th
    Cahill Thos, 1021 E Adams
    Cahill Edward, 713 S 8th
Cahill Thos, 713 S 12th
Call Jas, cor 12th and Edwards
Callin Nicholas, 404 W Mason
Callahan Mrs, 624 N 3d
Callahan Edward, 404 W Calhoun av
Callahan Peter, 421 W Mason
Caldwell David, E Madison bet 5th and 6th
Camp Miss Nancy, 619 N 1st
Camp Chas L, 1147 N 5th
Camp Mrs Alice, 407 W Mason
Campbell John R, S College bet Jackson and Edwards
Campbell A D, 825 S 3d
Campbell Wm, 933 S 2d
Campbell Wm, S 2d and Edwards
Campbell Jas, 917 E Capitol av
Campbell Matthew, 1206 E Adams
Cameron John, 924 E Miller
Canfield Henry, 623 W Monroe
Cannon Mrs M, se cor 10th and Cook
Cannon Chas, 415 E Monroe, up stairs
Canterbury R P, 116 S 2d
Cantrall Z G, N 2d n of Union
Cantrall L D, 112 W Allen
Canty Pat, 1203 E Capitol av
Capitol av house, 901 E Capitol av

Capps J T, 837 S 5th
Carman Wm H, 1212 S 7th
Carmean Robt, 302 W Carpenter
Carmody John, 114 N 6th, the old grocery store
Carpenter Geo, 531 N 7th
Carpenter A F, N 8th bet Bergen and N G av
Carpenter John, 1114 N Bond
Carpenter Buel, 601 W Capitol av
Carpenter Edward, 1220 S 4th
Carriel Miss Ester, 714 E Adams
Care Wm, 809 S 18th
Carlin Jas, ne cor W Cook and Spring
Carrigan Mrs Susan, 819 E Adams
Carrier Thos, 1224 E Adams
Carey Eva, 113 N 9th
Carroll Chas, 800 E Washington, up stairs
Carroll Hugh, 931 S 14th
Carter Rev J Robt, W Washington, near gas works
Carter Albert, 1404 E Monroe
Carter Geo, 1228 E Adams
Carter W S, 415 S 10th
Carter J W, 444 S 2d, U S Ex Agt
Carter Chas, 17th and S G av
Carter Anderson, 1404 E Monroe
Carver D W, 315 W Monroe
Casserly Peter, S 9th bet Edwards and Cook
Cassett C M, 406 W Edwards
Casey S V, 1613 E Mason
Casey Thos, cor 15th and Jackson
Castro Joseph, 1231 S 12th
Chaffee L A, S 9th bet Jackson and Edwards
Chaffee Owen, 1118 E Adams
Chalmers Wm, N 8th bet Bergen and N G av
Chandler Jas, N 8th bet Bergen and N G av
Chandler Geo, se cor 1st and Reynolds
Chapin Mrs Martha, 201 S Walnut
Chapin Wm, 725 S 12th
Chapman E, se cor 1st and Edwards
Chase Primus, 620 N 2d
Chase Hiram, N 1st bet Union and Pine
Charles Francis, sw cor 12th and Reynolds
Chatterton Geo W, 509 S 6th
Chenery John W, sw cor High and Pasfield
Chrust Chas, 1205 S 12th
Chulez Conrad, 419 N 2d
Church M B, 232 W Jackson
Chinn Wm, Reynolds bet 10th and 11th
Chinn Daniel, W William and Walnut
Clark Mrs W, 438 N 4th

Clark F, 1111 S 7th
Clark Henry & Co, 10th and Washington, saloon
Clark John, Lincoln bet 12th and 13th
Clark John, 1005 E Mason
Clark Robert, 644 N 3d
Clark S G, 1030 S 6th
Clark H F, 903 S 7th
Clark Mrs, 10th and Clay
. Clark John, E Washington bet 9th and 10th, saloon
Clark Frank, 1128 E Cook
Clark H R, 923 E Cook
Clark S S, S 7th bet Washington and Adams
Claspill S H, 409 W Capitol av
Claus A, 325 N 6th
Claus August, 630 N 7th
Clay Henry, 423 E Washington, up stairs
Clay John, N 10th bet Madison and Mason
Clay Henry, sw cor 12th and Washington
Claybourne W F, 709 S 11th
Clave F, 923 S 4th
Claven Pat, N Bond
Clear Pat, 1209 E Washington
Cleary Daniel, 229 N 2d
Cleverly B F, 105 N Doyle av
Clemmins Edward, cor 11th and Kansas
Clements Henry, 524 N 5th
Clevinger R T, 621 N 5th
Cleeber Anton, 358 W Carpenter
Cliber John, 1301 E Capitol av
Clifford Thos, 1112 N 4th
Closson Dr, 806 S 5th
Cloney Mrs Anna, 914 S 14th
Colbert Mrs H, 602 W Hay
Coats Abner, 528 N 8th
Coats Rufus, 1431 E Washington
Coats A, 1327 E Washington, grocer
Cobb R, E Washington bet 1st and 2d
Cochran H E, 1026 N 5th
Cochran Albert, 819 E Carpenter.
Coe L W, 903 S 4th
Cogdal W S, 927 E Cook
Cody T A, 722 S 13th
Coberly J, Madison bet 11th and 12th
Cole Geo C, 413 N 4th
Cole H W, 634 N 2d
Coles Edward, N 3d bet Carpenter and Union
Colebecker Peter, 916 S 11th
Colebecker Toney, 910 S 11th
Coleman Mrs L A, 438 N 4th

Coleman Ellis, Reynolds bet 11th and 12th
Coleman L H, nw cor Miller and 1st
Coleman T, 170 ; E Capitol av
Coleman Michael, 12th bet Clay and Kansas
Coleman Mrs, N 2d bet Washington and Jefferson
Coleman Geo, 10th bet Jefferson and Madison
Coleman Chas, 118 E Mason
Colgan Edward, Madison bet 12th and 13th
Colligan P, 235 N 14th
Colby W H, 1028 N 5th
Collier Mrs, Madison bet 8th and 9th
Collier N B, 812 E Reynolds
Colvin Lewis, 132 N 13th
Collins Pat, 1013 E Jefferson
Collins C, 730 N 7th
Collins W S, W Jefferson bet Doyle av and State
Collins Thos, 700 & 702 E Adams, boarding and saloon
Compton Peter, 1014 E Washington
Connell Mrs H, cor 15th and Clay
Conant P H, 722 S 5th
Conant Lee, 708 S 5th
Condell John, 605 S 4th
Condon Joseph, 1001 S 12th
Coulon P, sw cor Spring and Allen, grocer
Conlon Bartley, 1312 E Jackson
Conkling Clinton L, se cor Wright and Canedy
Conkling Wm J, 808 S 4th
Conkling J C, 801 S 6th
Connelly Terrence, 414 W Williams
Conolley M, 1229 E Madison
Connelly Mrs Mary, se cor 1st and Reynolds
Connelly Michael, 114 ; N 8th
Connelly Thos, 1219 E Madison
Connelly Will A, 508 S 8th
Connelly Mrs Anne, 510 N 5th
Connelly Mrs, 1417 E Capitol av
Connelly Geo S, 727 S 5th
Connor Wm, 224 N 11th
Conover Geo, Madison and 17th ns
Conner Mrs C, 722 E Madison
Conners Mrs Annie, cor 9th and Adams
Conners Michael, Bond and N G av
Conners David O, cor 15th and Cook
Connor E L, 201 W Capitol av
Conroy Martin, 1125 E Reservoir
Cotsch Mrs G, 319 W Edwards
Constant Geo, 210 W Edwards
Constant John W, 105 ws square, stereotyper
Constant A, 1209 S 7th

Consler Frank, 730 E Monroe
Converse B M, 1112 S 6th bet Scarritt and Allen
Conway Patrick, 1131 E Jefferson
Cook H F, se cor 3d and Canedy
Cook Thos, 324 N 6th
Cook Wm, ne cor Monroe and Doyle av
Cook Geo, 1102 N 7th
Cook Gen John, 206 E Adams
Cooney L, 603 W Calhoun av
Coon Levi, nw cor 9th and Division
Coon Mrs Sarah, 640 N 4th
Cooper Robt, S 3d bet Washington and Adams
Cooper John, 300 W Jefferson
Cooper Miss Lizzie, 114 E Edwards
Cooper Mrs, Mason bet 15th and 16th
Coffron Roy, 514 S College
Cothran Wm, se cor 3d and Madison
Correthers Green, 901 E Carpenter
Corson R H, 643 N 4th
Corey P M, 118 S Walnut
Corey Wm, 932 S 2d
Corby John, 1402 E Jackson
Corcoran Jas, 506 W Williams
Corkven Thos, 830 S 14th
Corderman Geo, 1000 S 11th
Corkery & Triebel, 105 N 5th, boots and shoes
Cottet Jules, 206 N 4th, machinist
Council Jas, 1020 S College
Court Robt, 1204 E Monroe
Courtwright Isaac D, ne cor Miller and Rutlegde
Couch Robt A, 1427 E Adams
Courtney John, 925 E Cook
Cowgill W B, Walnut bet Washington and Jefferson
Cowell A J, Madison bet 7th and 8th
Crabb Jas, nw cor Mason and 8th
Crafton John, 307 E Monroe
Crafton Thos, 523 N 6th
Craig Samuel, 1423 E Monroe
Craig John, 529 W Monroe
Craig Daniel, 925 S 12th
Craft Mrs, 404 N 5th
Cramp Matthew, 719 S 15th
Cramer L E, Edwards bet 12th and 13th
Crane Mrs M, 1204 E Jackson
Crane Patrick, 14th bet Jefferson and Madison
Creighton James A, 831 W Jefferson
Crie M, 116 N 13th
Christman Mat, 708 S 11th
Creasey ——, W State and W G av

Crissey Edgar, 306 W Wright
Creive Manuel, Carpenter bet 1st and 2d
Cresey A B, 1104 N Rutledge
Critchley Thos, N 2d bet Carpenter and Union
Crowley Mrs, 1208 E Madison
Cromwell C C, 724 E Mason
Crowder W A, 223 N 2d
Crossman Peter, 901 E Mason
Crook A N J, 514 E Capitol av
Crowell W D, 418 N 2d
Crawford John, 909 E Madison
Crobius Walter F, 1158 N 7th
Coyle John, 1016 S 2d
Crudden Nicholas, Mason and E G av
Cruser Emma, 1155 N 9th
Cruser Chas C, 510 N 4th
Crouse Rev B F, nw cor 6th and Madison
Culp W D, S 8th bet Allen and Vine
Culligan Mrs, 13th and Mason
Culp Mrs, cor 5th and Mason
Cullom Gov S M, S 4th bet Jackson and Edwards
Culver S M, sw cor 4th and Allen
Cummins Mat, 328 W Calhoun av
Culpan Herbert, 923 S Pasfield
Cunningham M, 1810 E Washington
Cunningham F N, 411 N 14th
Cunningham D N, 628 S 9th
Cunningham Mrs Mary, 520 S 7th
Cunningham Cormick, 540 W Williams
Cumberworth Henry, Reynolds bet 15th and 16th
Curran Thos, 1123 N Rutledge
Curran Michael, 518 W Calhoun av
Curran John, 520 W Mason
Curran John, 1425 E Cook
Currier J H, 1305 E Monroe
Currier S, 401 W Monroe
Curry Mrs O C, nw cor 4th and Canedy
Currington Samuel A, 820 S Pasfield
Cuthbert Wm, Reynolds bet 11th and 12th
Cusick John, 308 N 13th
Curtis Jas, Monroe bet 18th and E G av
Curtis Joel, 1627 E Jackson
Cubber John, 1230 S 11th
Cutright Wm, se cor 10th and Adams
Cutright Mrs S A, 923 S College
Cotter John, cor Cook and E G av

DAILY PAT, 515 N 2d
Daily Dennis, 614 S Walnut
Daily John, 120 W Carpenter
Daily Edward, 1025 E Washington
Daily Tim, 515 N 2d
Deber Lillie, 804 E Madison
Dalby Joel, N 3d S of N G av
Dallman Chas, 909 E Monroe
Debrah John, 355 W Reynolds
Dana F L & Co, board of trade rooms
Dana L D & Son, mill, se cor 7th and Jefferson
Dana L D, ne cor Walnut and Washington
Dana G S, 511 E Monroe, grocery
Day R F, 441 N 6th
Dana L E, 714 E Mason
Dana J S, 825 S 5th
Darcy John, 1024 N 5th
Daughton Wm, 17th and Adams
Daughton C, N 8th bet Bergen and N G av
Daughton John, 1157 N 8th
Daughton Chas, 1153 N 8th
Daugherty Margaret, N 8th bet Jefferson and Madison
David Mrs L, 820 S Spring
Dates G, 702 S Spring
Davis John, 912 E Miller
Davis Jas, cor Clay and Cass
Davis Mrs M, 402 S 6th
Davis Thos, 231 N 15th
Davis Mary A, sw cor 13th and Mason
Davis Thos, 1152 N 8th
Davis Dr K B, Walnut bet Washington and Jefferson
Davis Franklin, 301 W Jefferson
Davis Wm H, 214 W Capitol av
Davis Mrs E, 1st bet Washington and Jefferson
Davis J W, 6.9 E Adams
Davidson Henry B, sw cor 8th and Enos av
Davidson Mrs S W, 415 E Monroe, up stairs
Dawson N E, 913 south 1th
Dawson Richard, 525 N 4th
Day P H, 519 S Spring
Day W M, 817 E Adams
Day R F & Bro, 404 E Washington, feed store
Dayton Mrs, ne cor 11th and Madison
Dannerberger John, 220 W Mason
DeCamp John, 119 E Reynolds
DeCamp Chas, 1141 N 5th
DeCamp Wm, 615 E Reynolds
Death Jas A, 132 W Canedy
DeCastro Jos, 1043 N 6th

DeCrastes Sam, 1407 E Adams
DeCastro John, 200 N 13th
DeCrastes John, 1407 E Adams
Decker E B, 811 E Washington
Decker J J, 221 W Jackson
Dedrich Fred, 1059 N 6th
Dedling J B, 904 S 7th
Dee Thos, 442 W Carpenter
DeFrates Manuel, ne cor 14th and Mason
DeFrates Antony, 7th and Enos av
DeFrates Anton Zacria, N 13th and Jefferson
DeFrates F, N 13th bet Jefferson and Madison
DeFrates Edward, 1015 E Miller
DeFrates John, Miller bet 11th and 12th
DeFrates Manuel, 1105 E Miller
DeFrates Daniel, 1015 E Miller
DeFrates Joseph A, 310 N 14th
DeFrates Philip, Miller bet 11th and 12th
DeFrates J, 1123 N 8th
DeFrates Mary, 1019 E Mason
DeFrates Emanuel, sw cor 13th and Reynolds
DeFrates John, 1107 N 8th
DeFrates M, 1127 N 8th
DeFrates M A, 208 N 13th
DeFrates Henry, 1121 E Miller
DeFrates Antony, Miller bet 10th and 11th
DeFrates F A, 1223 E Jefferson
DeFrates Antone, se cor 14th and Madison
DeFrates J & Co, 831 E Reynolds
DeFrates Manuel, Miller bet 11th and 12th
DeFrates Antone, 14th bet Washington and Jefferson
Dehn Fred, 1104 N 6th
Diehr Chas, 529 N Klein
Deicken A F, 404 S 8th
Deill John, W Calhoun av w of 610
Deilig C, W Washington and John
Delany Pat, 15th and Jefferson
Delany Philip, 14th s of Clay
Delany Jas, sw cor 8th and Miller
Delany John, 1109 N Rutledge
Delany John C, 830 E Reynolds
Demattoes Frank, 1115 E Jefferson
Dempsey Mrs, 1131 E Washington
Dennis Henry, 314 N 14th
Denton Geo, N 4th near N G av
Dent Wm, Reynolds bet 11th and 12th
Denney Jas, 1318 E Washington
Derry Geo, 14th and Adams
—6

Derry John, 828 E Miller
DeSanno Jas, 818 S 13th
Desel John, W Reynolds bet Klein and Rutledge
Desmond Denis, W Mason between 1st and Klein
DeSantos Anto, 405 N 14th
DeSilva John, 102 E Washington
Detrick Ben, 555 W Jefferson
Dapron Lewis, 411 W Jefferson
Davenport Thos, se cor 3d and Union
Devault F M, 715 N 2d
Devlin Edward, 1300 E Edwards
Devereaux Mrs, 329 S 4th
DeVerra Mrs Mary, 616 N 2d
DeVares D A, N 9th bet Reynolds and Carpenter
Deyo Lewis, se cor 5th and Scarritt
Deyo Noah, 526 S 8th
Dickins Cicero, 821 S 15th
Dickerman & Co, 422 S 4th, woolen mills
Dickerman H S, 941 S 4th
Dickey Wm, 603 S College
Dickson Andrew, 215 W Washington
Diller R W, 431 S 7th
Diller Z R, Carpenter west end
Dillon John, 15th bet Jefferson and Madison
Dinkel L, 1220 E Monroe
Dinkel Margaret, 310 W Mason
Dirksen Anton, 1010 E Cook
Dirksen, 716 E Mason
Divilbiss Noah, 506 N 5th
Dixon Dr J N, 419 E Washington
Dobbins Nicholas, cor 14th and Jackson
Dockson Edward, 108 W Madison
Dockson Chas, 1217 E Jackson
Dodge L T, 12th and N G av
Dodge Miss Nancy, W Jefferson and New
Dodds, 554 S 11th
Dodds Mrs A R, 720 E Mason
Doenges A, nw cor Capitol av and Spring
Donlon M, 304 N 13th
Donovan Wm, 1143 N 1st
Donohue Thos, 728 E Washington
Donlon Mrs, 302 N 13th
Donovan Thos, 704 S 14th
Donnegan Geo W, 1038 S 3d
Donnegan W, E Washington bet 9th and 10th
Donnovan John, 439 W Reynolds
Donegan Thos, Mason bet 15th and 16th
Downey Mrs Annie, 818 E Carpenter
Donnegan Mrs, 225 E Carpenter

Donnovan P, 416 W Carpenter
Donnelly Wm, 509 N 7th
Donnell Mrs, 1177 N 9th
Donnelly John, Carpenter bet 11th and 12th
Douglas John, 932 S 14th
Doul Mrs, 411 and 413 E Washington
Doren Mrs E, 714 N 7th
Douglas John, 819 E Carpenter
Douglas Henry, 18th and Cass
Dowe O E, ne cor 7th and Allen
Dowe John, 1016 E Washington
Dowery Mrs, 223 N 15th
Downey John, nw cor W Washington and John
Downey John, 929 E Carpenter
Downs Wm, Reservoir bet 11th and 12th
Dougherty Daniel, 1022 E Madison
Dowken John, N 2d n of Union
Dowdel Geo, 1013 S College
Doyle Michael, W Governor and W G av
Doyle John, 1717 E Adams
Doyle Martin, 922 E Monroe
Doyle Maurice, ne cor 8th and Reynolds
Doyle Thos, 1204 E Jefferson
Doyle Pat, 1711 E Capitol av
Dubois N, 518 N 5th
Duggins Mrs M J, Madison bet 7th and 8th
Duggin —, 1107 S 12th
Duggin Dan, 1105 S 12th
Duffey Jas, 710 E Madison
Duff H, 1730 E Capitol av
Duff Wm H, 1509 E Mason
Dunham A, 1125 E Madison
Dudley Mrs M, Miller bet 11th and 12th
Dunham —, 205 N 2d
Dunlap W N, 516 S 10th
Dunlap A, 435 S New
Dunbar Frank, 826 S 3d
Duncan Clark, 312 N 13th
Dunning Wm, 118 W Edwards
Dunning A J, 826 S 4th
Dunham John, 220 W Mason
Dunham C J, S 18th
Dunn Thomas, se cor 9th and Edwards
Dunn Mrs, cor 7th and Douglas
Du Pleaux Thomas, N 4th bet Carpenter and Union
Durkin Jas, 500 se cor Washington and New
Durkin P, 617 E Washington
Drake Wm, nw cor 9th and Capitol av
Durkson Frank, S 12th

Dressendorffer Wm, 1401 E Cook
Draude Lewis, 138 W Jefferson
Dressendorffer, 313 W Cook
Dresser Dr T W, 300 E Monroe
Dresch John, 514 W Carpenter
Drury P, 511 E Jefferson, boarding
Drury Tobe, Mason bet 11th and 12th
Drury Jas, 827 S 5th
Drone Issac, 206 Elliott av
Drummond Mrs Mary, 620 N 3d
Dwyre David, 1716 E Adams

EADS O P, E Canedy bet 3d and 4th
  Eagan Mrs, 113 S 6th, up stairs
    Eastman A, 615 S 6th
Eastman S F, sw cor 6th and Elm
Earley L, 709 E Jefferson
Eaton Page, 909 S 5th
Eberlen Jacob, 938 N 3d
Eckus Henry W, N 2d bet Carpenter and Union
Eckled John, 112 N 13th
Eck Geo, Edwards bet 10th and 11th
Eck John, 1013 E Reynolds
Eck Mrs, 717 E Reynolds
Eddy Nick, 625 E Adams
Edmands Chas H, 414 W Edwards
Edmands Chas, 507 S College
Edwards A, S 5th bet Capitol av and Jackson
Edwards Mrs, 305 S 5th, up stairs
Edwards B S, Union bet 4th and 5th
Edwards N W, S 2d s of State House
Edwards J B, cor 18th and Jackson
Edwards Jacob, 314 N 10th
Edwards J B, nw cor Madison and 13th
Eifert John D, Edwards and E G av
Eielson Aslag, 603 N 7th
Elder Chas A, 710 N 5th
Elder S S, south 8th bet Cass and Clay
Eldridge Harmon, Elliott av
Eldridge Hugh, cor 14th and Capitol av
Elkin Dick, 503 S W G av
Elkin G, 823 S 4th
Elkin Chas, 1015 S Spring
Elkin E S, 310 W Monroe
Elkin Wm F, 222 E Wright
Elliott Temp, 835 S 6th

Ellis David, 17th and Clay
Ellis Maria, 1110 E Reynolds
Ellis Yates, 502 N 12th
Ellis Geo, 331 W Mason
Elshoff, 630 S 11th
Elsey Jas, 1130 E Monroe
Elfgen Mrs E, 1008 S 13th
Ehman Martin, 909 S 12th
Emmons Lucinda, 1220 E Jefferson
Engel P, 200 E Jefferson
Engle John, Miller bet 8th and 9th
English Turney, 1022 E Washington
Engelskirchen Henry, 505 W Monroe
Enos Z A, 434 N 2d
Ennels Mrs, 2d bet Washington and Jefferson
Ensel A, ne cor 4th and Madison
Ensel L S, 625 S 7th
Enz F, 103 E Carpenter
Enos Mrs Susan P, 730 N 6th
Erickson Mrs, 316 W Edwards
Erickson Henry, 414 N 2d
Eslinger J E, 1514 E Capitol av
Etter Geo, N 1st n of Miller
Ettelbrick August, cor 11th and Edwards
Evans Geo, 620 N 5th
Evans John, 900 S Spring
Evans J B, 4th bet Washington and Adams
Evans Wm, N 6th bet Bergen and Elm
Euber Mrs Margaret, W Reynolds w of 427 .
Ewart A, 924 S 11th

FAGAN JAS, 1102 E Washington
Fanning Patrick, 1326 E Adams
Faith Mrs R Mary, 711 E Adams
Farley Jas, 911 E Adams
Farmer Mrs Mary, 11th and Clay
Farley John, N G av w of Rutledge
Farley Mrs L, cor 14th and Capitol av
Farris Toney, 826 E Miller
Farris Wm, 400 W Adams
Farrill Edward S, 15th s of Douglas
Fayart Peter, 620 S 9th
Fayart A, 722 E Reynolds
Fayart H, 1201 S 4th
Fawcett A, ne cor 6th and Madison
Fehr Chas, 612 E Washington, saloon and restaurant
Feitshans F R, 808 S 2d

Feitshans Prof J C, 323 S 5th, elocution
Felber Jacob, 15th and Jefferson
Feldkamp & Son, 320 E Washington, dye works
Feltham Thos G, 230 W Capitol av
Ferguson Samuel, Jefferson bet 7th and 8th
Ferguson Mrs E, 211 N 15th
Fernandes Manuel, 1101 N 6th
Fernandes A, Madison bet 9th and 10th
Fernandes Joseph, 1125 E Miller
Fernandes John J, 1109 E Mason
Fernandes John, 311 N 4th
Fernandes Manuel jr, 1101 N 6th
Fernandes John, cor Reservoir and 11th
Fernandes N, sw cor Klein and Calhoun av
Fernandes John F, 1201 E Washington
Fero Joseph, 1111 E Mason
Fereira J, E Carpenter bet 1st and 2d
Fereira Mrs Levina, 221 E Carpenter
Fero Mrs Mary, 313 N 10th
Ferril Edward, 220 S 4th
Ferril John, se cor Edwards and Spring
Ferris Geo D, 713 N 7th
Fessenden Mrs, 623 N 5th
Fetzer Fred, 1125 N 7th
Fetzer Philip, 714 N 6th
Feuerbacher Fred, 125 W Calhoun av
Fidler H M, 420 W Mason
Fidengruber M, 438 West Carpenter
Figwera Nicholas, 900 E Mason
Fielder R A, S Pasfield bet Allen and Vine
Figuera Manuel, E Washington bet 8th and 9th
Finley T, cor 8th and Capitol av
Finley Wm E, Capitol av bet 14th and 15th
Fisher M A, 426 W Adams
Fisher Mrs S B, 727 N 7th
Fisher A H, W Monroe bet Spring and College
Fields Mrs Vian, 224 N 11th
Fisher Wm, 417 N 4th
Fisher S D, 200 W Jackson
Fisher Chas, 305 S 5th, wire works
Fisk W H, 1004 N 5th
Fitzgerald John, 311 W Jefferson
Fitzgerald John, 1162 N 4th
Fitzgerald Patrick, 112 W Jefferson
Fitzgerald Jas M, se cor 7th and Allen
Fitzgerald Pat, 1125 N Rutledge
Fitzgerald P, N 8th bet Division and N G av
Fitzgerald M, 218 W Mason
Fitzgibbon Jas, 425 W Mason

Fitzpatrick P. nw cor Cook and Spring
Fitzpatrick Thos, W Canedy w of College
Fitzpatrick Thos, 12th and N G av
Fitzpatrick John, 1132 N 5th
Fitzpatrick Jas, N 5th s of N G av
Fitzpatrick Philip, 111 W Cook
Fitzpatrick J E, 515 E Washington, saloon
Fitzsimmons M, 1830 E Washington
Fitzsimmons Jas, 1214 E Madison
Fixmer John P, 131 E Jefferson
Flegler Mrs A H, 114 E Madison
Flager, N 2d bet Carpenter and Union
Flaherty Edward, 827 E Madison
Flanagan John, 1708 E Washington
Flanagan C, 217 N 9th
Flanks Annie, N 8th bet Washington and Jefferson
Flemming Jas, Adams bet 10th and 11th
Fletcher A, 429 W Mason
Fletcher Mrs C, 1300 E Washington
Fleming ——, 203 East Washington
Fleury Frank, 505 E Washington
Fleck Chas, 429 W Mason
Flood Annie, 1031 E Adams
Flood Mrs Mary, 909 E Madison
Florville Wm, 118 S 11th
Floyd J Q A, 1312 E Monroe
Flower John, 14th bet Madison and Mason
Florey Adam, W Miller w end
Flynn Thos G, 208 W Mason
Flynn Michael, 824 S Spring
Flynn Thos, nw cor 12th and Madison
Flynn John, 115 W Wright
Flynn Patrick, 909 E Adams
Flynn Wm, W Madison w of Rutledge
Flynn Wm J, W Reynolds bet 1st and Klein
Fogarty Mrs Annie, 1124 E Madison
Fogarty John, 1031 N 6th
Fogarty Jas, 1017 E Washington
Fogarty Mrs M, 1221 E Capitol av
Fogle Peter, 1150 N 6th
Foley M, 1154 N 7th
Foley M, 1110 N 7th
Foley John, se cor Reynolds and Rutledge
Foley M, 225 S Doyle av
Foley Mrs Alice, cor E G av and Cass
Foley Wm C, 717 E Mason
Foley Mrs Mary, 316 W Reynolds
Fooshce Mrs Annie, sw cor 4th and Carpenter
Forbes Joseph, 700 E Union

Ford Mrs Sarah, 315 S 5th, boarding house
Ford Wesley, 501 W Monroe
Ford Edward, 227 E Carpenter
Ford John, Mason bet 15th and 16th
Forden J M, 911 S 4th
Forman Frank, Capitol av bet 15th and 16th
Fortado Toney, 1104 E Madison
Forrester P C, 1044 N 5th
Forsythe A, 1514 E Mason
Fosselman J B, 302 E Scarritt
Foster Joseph, 113 W Cook
Foster Wm, 214 E Carpenter
Foster John, 1005 E Jefferson
Foster Henry, nw cor New and Edwards
Foster Henry, 832 S Spring
Foster N, 423 W Reynolds
Foster A H, ne cor Monroe and New
Fortune L, 706 E Washington
Fortune John, 1119 E Jefferson
Fortney David, 509 S 11th
Fountain Theo, 1216 E Edwards
Fowler Mrs E N, 215 E Adams
Fowler Mrs R H, 807 S 2d
Fowler Dr E S, se cor 2d and Cook
Fox M L, 117 N 4th, up stairs
Fox B F, 819 N 3d
Francis Vincent, 331 N 14th
Frank M, 14th between Jefferson and Madison
Frank John, 14th bet Jefferson and Madison
Frank John, 1100 E Miller
Frank A, 1121 E Miller
Franklin John, 900 E Monroe
Franz Baptist, 508 W Mason
Frazer Wm, 121 W Mason
Fraive Gus, 426 N 10th
Freitag Chas, 806 E Enterprise
Freidinger Henry, Enterprise bet 10th and 11th
Fredricks Robt, 806 S 12th
Friedrich John, 520 E Jefferson, Humboldt House
Fredricks Wm, ne cor 9th and Lincoln
Free Conrad, 548 W Mason
Fredman Simon, ne cor Allen and Henrietta
Frederick John, W Herndon w of Bond
Freire Manuel, Lincoln bet 11th and 12th
Fruechtal Mrs C, 228 W Carpenter
Freund John, 110 E Madison
Freeman C W, 704 W Monroe
Freeman Mrs Malvina, 219 W Madison
Freeman J H, S 7th bet Jackson and Edwards

Freeman Wm, 312 N 2d
Freeman N L, 905 S 6th
French A W, se cor Monroe and Pasfield
French Herman, 1228 E Adams
French Webb, cor 5th and Jefferson, up stairs
French Herman, 1230 E Adams
French C G, se cor 3d and Wright
Frey & Hartmann, 613 E Monroe
Frisbie Wm, 122 E Reynolds
Friedman A, 410 S 8th
Frounfelter Mrs A J, 312 N 6th
Fry Adam, S 12th
Fry Mrs Annie, 423 E Washington
Fry Jacob, 1323 S 12th
Fry Mrs L, 905 E Carpenter
Fudge Geo, 504 S 11th
Fudge Sam, 508 S 11th
Fudge Adam, 1120 E Jackson
Fuller A S, 417 W Monroe
Fuller Frank, 1021 N 5th
Fuller Mrs S, 11th and Douglas
Fultz Joseph H, 1170 N 4th
Funk Henry, 138 N 13th
Furlong Jas, 128 S 6th
Furlong P, 916 E Miller

GABEL MRS, nw cor 7th and Miller
Gable M, sw cor Spring and Allen
Gaffagan Jas, 334 W Carpenter
Gaffagan M, 629 East Washington
Gabert A F, 811 E Capitol av
Gage M, S 7th bet Capitol av and Jackson
Gaffeny John, Washington bet 17th and 18th
Gaffeny B, 326 S Doyle av
Gaffney Dr E C, 122 N 6th
Gall G, 315 W Madison
Gall Fred, cor 9th and Miller
Gallagher Miss E, 1119 E Jackson
Gallagher Hugh, 103 W Cook
Galligan Thos, N 7th N of Bergen
Gallagher Pat, 416 E Madison
Gallagher Jas, 403 S 4th
Gallaher Mrs Margaret, 8th bet Scarritt and Allen
Gamble Mrs M E, 116 (old No.) N 5th
Gannon Patrick W, 424 William st
Gannon Mrs Mary, 556 W Washington
Gardner Wm L, 312 N 5th
Garo Hammon, 359 W Reynolds
—7

Gardner C W, 511 & 513 N S square
Gardner Jas S, 1129 N 5th
Gardner Jas, 923 E Mason
Gardner Mrs P, 435 W Edwards
Galvin Dan, Mason bet 16th and 17th
Garland Mrs Lucy, 220 S 4th, boarding
Garland Jas M, se cor 5th and Miller
Garland A M, 813 W Jefferson
Garr John, 1223 S 15th
Gaa & Fleck, Washington bet 4th and 5th, barbers
Gaa Peter, 401 W Reynolds
Garr Geo, 1330 E Brown
Gaise Louis, N 8th bet Carpenter and Miller
Garms ——, se cor of N and W G av
Garinstead Wesley, 409 W Allen
Gartling Lawrence, 18th and Adams
Gartling Mrs Margaret, 716 S 14th
Garton Geo, 942 S Spring
Gart A N, 11th bet Madison and Mason
Gertiser Frank A, 1105 E Mason
Garvin Dan, 1212 E Monroe
Garvey Patrick, nw cor Carpenter and Rutledge
Gaude Emile, 329 S 4th
Gevey M, 1131 N 8th
Geering Geo, 933 N 3d
Gehring Phillip, W Herndon w of Rutledge
Geathers Mrs, 809 E Washington
Geathers Frank, 1019 E Mason
Geathers Richard, Carpenter bet 15th and 16th
Geathard John, 724 W Washington
Geathard David, 724 W Washington
Geathard John, 100 W Washington
Gephart Mr, Adams bet 10th and 11th
George J, 17th and S G av
Gehlman Geo S, 327 S Doyle av
Gehlman S H, W Capital av bet College & Pasfield
Gehlman E F, 119 S Walnut
Gehlman E, E Jefferson bet 4th and 5th, shop
Gehrmann C A, 1021 N 3d and Pine
Gehring Fred, E Jefferson bet 4th and 5th
Geist Lewis, cor 13th and Douglas
Gerhart Fred, 1211 S 12th
Geisner Mrs E, 145 (old No) W Carpenter
German Mrs, 1016 S Spring
Gibbons Geo, 120 W Wright
Giblin Mrs P, se cor 5th and Carpenter
Gielbe M, 312 W Carpenter
Giese A, 1225 E Washington
Gillmore W J, 424, W Williams

Gillmore Hugh, cor 18th and Washington
Gillman Perry, Madison bet 2d and 3d
Gill Thos, 1114 N 4th
Gill Joseph A, 101 Washington and 5th
Gilliam E T, 1101 E Miller
Gilliam F A, 1101 E Miller
Gilliland Wm A, 1202 E Capitol av
Gilliland J B, 1412 E Jackson
Gilliland W H, E Mason bet 7th and 8th
Gillock Mrs Nancy, Miller bet Klein and Rutledge
Girard Clements, 1162 N 8th
Glasgow Alexander, 408 W. Washington
Glass Geo, 508 W Carpenter
Glass Geo, 358 W Carpenter
Glass John, 235 W Edwards
Glavan Marks, Elliott av and Walnut
Glancy M, sw cor Mason and Klein
Glover Chas, 15th North of Mason
Glynn Michael, 422 W Adams
Glysson Chas W, nw cor New and High
Gobble C A, cor Reynolds and Rutlege
Godley Frank, E Jeff. bet 3d and 4th, rag warehouse
Godley Frank, 1224 E Jefferson
Godey Henry, 712 South 12th
Goggin James, 906 S 11th
Golden Wm, 1058 N 5th
Goldschmidt G, 401 W Capitol av
Goldfuss P, 314 W Mason
Goldstein A, ne cor 9th and Madison
Goltra Dr J T, 506 W Monroe
Gomes Frank, 1019 E Miller
Gomes Manuel, 1227 E Jefferson
Gomes John, 123 N 13th
Gomes Lewis, 1105 E Miller
Gomes Joseph 712 E Jefferson
Gomes Antony, 522 N 10th
Gomes A, 210 E Carpenter
Gomes M, 9th and Lincoln
Gomes Joseph, 718 N 11th
Gonsalves John, 710 N 11th
Gonsalves J, 1110 E Mason
Gonse G, ne cor 9th and Adams
Godenrath John, 412 E Monroe, wagon shop
Gough Geo, 121 W Wright
Godenrath, 326 W Adams
Goodman Jacob, N 7th n of Bergen
Good Mrs, 422 S 11th
Goeden John M, 1024 E Reynolds

Goodwin John, 104 N 10th, saloon
Goodwin John, 1163 N 4th
Good Wm H, cor 6th and N G av
Goodwin Wm A, 610 S 11th
Gordon Mariah, 806 E Adams
Gordon B A, 1203 S 5th
Gordon A, N 5th bet Reynolds and Mason
Gordon Wm, 312 N 2nd
Gordon Mrs Mary, ne cor 3d and Capitol av
Gordon G W M, 1106 E Jackson
Gordon G W M, 500 S 11th, Grocery
Gordon A, 931 S 3d
Gordon Edward, 404 W Williams
Gorman Thos, 100 N 13th
Gorman Mrs, 1228 E Edwards
Gorman Pat, 1207 E Washington, saloon
Gorum Robt H, 40J W Williams
Gore Henry, W Vine w of Spring
Gore Micheal, ne cor 5th and Vine
Gottschalk Fred Mason, bet 16th and 17th
Gottschalk Mrs Mary, 214 W Cook
Gottschalk Wm, 214 W Cook
Gotsch Benjamin, W Jackson and Pasfield
Gough Geo, 408 S 4th
Gourley A F, nw cor Capital av and Lewis
Gourley J T, North Doyle av n of Washington
Goveia John, 1003 E Miller
Goveia John, 1013 E Carpenter
Goveia Aatonia, Lincoln bet 12th and 13th
Grady Martin, 1025 S 1st
Graeser Chas, cor 5th and Madison
Graeff Geo, 410 N 4th
Grab John, ne cor 5th and Carpenter
Grabach Wm, 570 W Elliott av and Walnut
Graham W M, 226 W Allen
Graham Jas, 306 W Adams
Graham Rev Mr, S 5th bet Vine and S G av
Graham Chas, 321 W Monroe
Graham Mrs Marget, W Capital av bet New and Walnut
Graham Mrs R, 500 S 7th
Grannels Mrs, 1524 E Washington
Grant Thos, 127 W Mason
Grant S D, 223 S 3d
Grant Dennis, 708 E Mason
Grant Jas, 439 N 4th
Grant Mrs S A, 112 E Jefferson
Grant H, 616 E Adams, tin store
Grant S D, 417 E Monroe, grocer

Grant Jas, 314 W Adams
Grant D, nw cor 8th and Vine
Graves B S, 224 S 6th, farmers' eating house
Gray Green, 817 E Carpenter
Gray Issac, 15th bet Jefferson and Madison
Gray Dr J N, 815 E Adams
Gray David, 307 N 15th
Gray Issac H, 411 S 7th, or 422 S 6th, new house
Gray Mrs, 1140 N 6th
Gray F, cor 18th and Cook
Gray Henry, N 15th n of Mason
Gray John 917 S 2d
Gray Mrs L A, S Pasfield bet Allen and Vine
Grebe John, se cor 12th and Reynolds
Gresch Chas, cor 11th and Cook
Gresch Chas, cor 11th and Cook, meat market
Green Geo W, 1006 S College
Green J R, 724 E Adams
Green C W, sw cor 5th and Cook
Green Wm, W Jackson bet College and Pasfield
Green Mrs Hannah, cor Walnut and N G av
Green Mrs C, 1024 S 11th
Green S H, 6th and Mason
Greenwood John, E Jackson bet 13th and 14th
Greenwood Wm V, 423 N 7th
Greenhalch J, 1205 E Capitol av
Gregory A M, 609 N 5th
Griffin Patrick 515 S New
Griffith B M, 618 S 6th
Griffith Miss H G, 214 S 6th, restaurant
Griffith H G, 211 S 5th, hair goods
Griffith D, E Carpenter bet 15th and 16th
Grimsley Wm P, 1002 S 4th
Griner E G, 1322 E Jackson
Grissom Mrs S, ne cor 4th and Capitol av
Gross Wm L 838 S 4th
Gross Mrs Mary, 908 E Madison
Gross Mrs E L, se cor 4th and Canedy
Gross & Conkling 224 S 5th
Groesbeck C, 710 N 6th
Grosspitz A, 722 S College
Grout J M, 1039 S 4th
Grossell Michael, 1102 cor Rutlege and Elliott av
Grubey Mrs M, 1222 E Mason
Grubb H B, 210 W Edwards
Gruenwald Otto, N 1st n of Miller
Gusswein Martin, ne cor Walnut and Williams
Gunn John H, N 6th bet Washington and Jefferson

Gunn Mrs, 405 E Monroe, up stairs
Guyer G H, 100 E Carpenter
Geist Anton, cor 13th and Cook
Gwynn David, 637 N 5th
Gwynn Wm, cor Walnut and N G av
Geyer Chas, cor 8th and Lincoln

HADLEY ROBT, 130 W Madison
Hagen M, 627 E Washington, up stairs
Hagermann Mrs. A, 12th bet Mason and Reynolds
Hagen M, 716 E Madison
Hagerty P, se cor 4th and N G av
Hagney Jas, 1128 E Madison
Hahn Chas, 627 N Klein, meat market
Hahn Geo, 1008 E Miller
Hahn John, 819 E Miller
Hahn L H & Co, 411 E Monroe, meat market
Hahn Chas, 631 N Klein
Hailey Mrs, 112 W Madison
Hain Hugo, 1113 S 11th
Haynes A, 9th bet Enos av and Lincoln
Haines Mrs Mary, S 4th bet Monroe and Capitol av
Haines Frank, S 3d cor Scarritt and Allen
Haines Henry, 1319 E Washington
Halberg Wm, ne cor Carpenter and Klein
Halfen Jacob, 519 N 6th
Hale Rev A, 221 E Adams
Hall Thos, 9th bet Adams and Monroe, horse shoeing
Hall Thos, 1401 E Capitol av
Hall O W, 1126 S Pasfield
Hall Joseph, 322 S 4th
Hall Ben, 529 S 12th
Hall C A, S 5th bet Allen and Vine
Hall J C, 316 W Monroe
Hall David 816 S 11th
Hall Henry, nw cor 8th and Allen
Hall Dr J G, ne cor 2d and Capitol av
Halligan Thos 1213 E Monroe
Hallahan Daniel O, 412 W Washington
Hallowell Joseph, 824 S 3d
Haltmann Joseph, 917 E Cook
Hamer Mrs L A, 616 S 5th, dress making
Hamer G W, 1025 S 8th
Hamer John G, 1209 E Capitol av
Hamilton L F, 512 N 7th
Haman Samuel, ne cor 1st and Reynolds
Hamlin E D, 630 S 5th

Hamilton Wm, N 4th bet Carpenter and Union
Ham Joseph, 1109 E Mason
Hammerslough, se cor 5th and Carpenter
Hampel Valentine, S Spring bet Scarritt and Wright
Haman F W, 303 W Jackson
Hammond J B, S 7th bet Scarritt and Allen
Hammon Thos, 1428 E Adams
Hammon Geo, 413 W Reynolds
Hampton S C, sw cor 5th and Wright
Hampton A, Mason and E G av
Hampton Mrs J, 817 S 4th
Handley Mrs Fred, 425 W Adams
Handy Thos, 709 E Adams, Grocer
Hankins Wm N, 1003 S College
Hankins 1003 S 2nd
Hand Mrs Julia, 807 E Adams
Hanley Peter, 924 S 13th
Hanlon B, 1207 E Madison, grocer
Hannon N B, 430 S 7th
Hansell J P, 1033 S 4th
Hanaphel Wm, cor Spring and Allen
Hannigan Wm, W Mason bet Klein and Rutledge
Hanratty O, 1208 E Monroe
Hancock W B, 315 E Adams
Hanson Mrs R, 1102 E Reynolds
Hanselman M, 600 N 7th
Hanratty O, 326 S 6th, gas fitting
Harbauer Frank, jr, 409 E Monroe
Harbauer Frank, sen, 412 E Adams
Harbauer C, 125 N 5th, saloon
Harbold Mrs, 1106 N 1st
Hardcastle Mrs Joseph, 717 S Spring, grocery
Harbison J C, 1117 E Jackson
Hardin Ben J, 521 E monroe, singer sewing machine
Hardin Ben J, 206 S Doyle av
Hartfelter M, W Madison bet Klein and Rutlege
Hardtner Dr J, 1016 S 6th
Hartley Greenwood, 11th and Enterprise
Hardin John J, sw cor Monroe and College
Hare Henry, N 14th s of Mason
Hargrave R H, 116 E Madison
Harlan Mrs M C, 1124 S 6th
Harris A J, cor 15th and Capitol av
Harris D P, 315 N 4th
Harris Martin, E Cook and G av
Haris M A, 429 N Klein
Harris Mrs M, 1104 S Spring
Harris Wm, ne cor 5th and Carpenter

Harris Mrs, 412 S 11th
Harris Levi, 1119 E Washington
Harris Dr N, 529 W William
Harris John, 1035 S Spring
Harrison Lewis, 219 W Jackson
Harrower Mrs J, 1028 E Monroe
Harney Martin, 1115 E Madison
Harving Henry, 1136 N 6th
Hart Miss Nellie, N 11th bet Madison and Mason
Harts P W, 509 N 5th
Harts P W, 223 S 5th, drug store
Hart John G, S 8th bet Edwards and Cook
Hartman Mrs M, 404 S 11th
Hart Miss H, 1202 E Jefferson
Hart Owen, 818 E Washington
Hartman Fred, 1117 E Monroe
Hartnett Morris, 1220 E Edwards
Hartman John, 909 E Mason
Harwood H R, 1017 E Monroe
Harwood, 1221 E Jackson
Hashman John, 1021 S 1st
Hatch O M, 1005 N 7th
Hatry Chas, Monroe bet 12th and 13th
Happy R J, N 9th bet Division and N G av
Hecht Samuel, 437 N 5th
Hatcher Wm, 919 E Carpenter
Hatfield Mrs E, 625 N 2d
Haughey M F, 1032 S Spring
Haughey Thos J, ne cor College and Allen
Hauck Mrs A, 13th and Reservoir
Hawley Issac, 422 S 5th
Hawley and Grant, 219 S 6th, up stairs, insurance agts
Hawley E B, 423 N 7th
Hawley Thos, 204 E Carpenter
Hawthorn Henry, 13th bet Cass and Clay
Hayes Miss Katie, 221 E Monroe, milliner
Hay, Greene and Littler, over 1st national bank, att'ys
Hay Miss, 328 S 8th
Hay Milton, S 4th bet Cook and Wright
Hay John, 14th and N G av
Hay Chas E, 821 S 2nd
Hay M, W Hay
Hays Simon, 500 N Bond
Hayden A, 1017 N 9th
Hayden W H, 324 W Jackson
Hayes Mrs John, 500 W Calhoun av
Haynie Mrs Z N, 1119 S 6th
Haywood Judge, 811 E Jefferson
Hazlett & Kane, 229 S 6th, attorneys

Hazlett Virgil, 517 W G av
Head Wm, 1026 E Mason
Healy Bernard, 923 S 14th
Heatherman John, 1147 N 7th
Heaton Geo, 1117 E Madison
Heddenburgh Geo, 928 S 5th
Hebberling T H, 1017 S College
Hecht R, 103 N 5th, cigars and tobacco
Heckler Ben, 320 W Madison
Heckley F, 417 S 11th
Heitele Joseph, 422 W Carpenter
Heidenreich A, 718 S College
Heimlich J, 204 S 6th, barber shop
Heimberger L, 100 W Washington, grocer
Hegele Pat, se cor 6th and N G av, meat market
Heselmyer August, 1011 N 4th
Hegele Pat, ne cor 6th and Reynolds, meat market
Hagerman Henry 709 N 7th
Heffern M, N 7th n of Bergen
Helfer Philip, 1227 S 11th
Hellweg R, nw cor Monroe and Walnut
Hellweg & Snape, 414 E Monroe, plumbers
Helmbrechts M, se cor Canedy and College
Helmle C A, N 4th bet Madison and Mason
Helmle Geo H, 5th and Jackson, architect
Helmle Wm, 428 S 5th, wood carver
Helleson Emel, 532 W Mason
Hemminger Martin, 631 Hay
Hemmick Jas M, 512 S 8th
Hender Louis, 206 S 6th, barber shop
Henderson Chas, N 1st bet Reynolds and Carpenter
Henning Dr T S, 426 S 6th
Henkle Nicholas, 1101 S 5th
Henkle Mrs J C, 819 S 5th
Henkle A, 932 S 5th
Henley Geo P, 619 S 7th
Hennesey Thos, 526 W Hay
Hennesey Jas, 827 S 13th
Henson John E, 1541 E Mason
Henson John, 816 N 2d
Henney W C, 804 S 11th
Henry Jas, 14th bet Washington and Jefferson
Henry Thos, ne cor Doyle av and Governor
Henry Wm, 813 S 12th
Hendricks Wm, S 12th bet Capitol av and Jackson
Henshaw John, sw cor 1st and Jefferson
Hermann Jacob, cor 11th and Douglas
Hefmann Robt, 201 W Mason, tin shop
—8

Hermann, C A, jr, ne cor Spring and Vine
Herman Chas, 818 E Monroe
Herman C A. sen, 950 S Spring, carpet weaver
Herndon & Colby, 105 ws square, attorneys
Herndon R F & Co, 512 ss square
Herndon R F, 904 S 5th
Herndon E B, 217 N 4th
Herndon L W, 112 W Madison
Hendon Mrs E, 802 E Adams
Herrick J E K, 8.5 S 4th
Hall & Herrick, 130 es square, clothing house
Heshing Detrick, 1123 S 12th
Hess John, nw cor Bond and Herndon
Hess Sol, 1215 E Jefferson
Hess Geo, cor 18th and Douglas
Hesser Geo, ne cor 8th and Adams
Hibbs Jas M, 419 N 6th
Hibbs Jas M, 32. S 6th, merchant tailor
Hibbard Geo, 901 E Capital av. hotel
Highfield John, 13th and Lincoln
Hickey Mrs Bridget, 201 S Doyle av
Hickey David, se cor Adams and College
Hicklin H, 326 N 13th
Hickman Dr W A, 331 N 5th
Hickox S W, Ill mills, cor 3d and Washington
Hickox Mrs, 618 S 7th
Hickox D, 912 E Adams, excelsior mills
Hickox Douglas, 628 and 630 S 7th
Hickox Volney, 1224 E Monroe
Hickox F, jr, 1008 E Adams
Hickox E R, 700 S 7th
Hickox F, sr, 1008 E Adams
Hicks, 1506 E Dapitol av
Higgins O, Reservoir bet 11th and 12th
Higgins Thos, 1219 E Washington
Higgins J M, 613 N 5th
Higgins E L, S 4th s of Allen
Higgins Robt, 918 S 5th
Higgins A D, S 4th bet Allen and Vine
Higgins Dr J A, 112 W Monroe
Higgins Patrick, 622 N 4th
Hill Robt, S 4th bet Allen and Scarritt
Hill Jas L, 1012 S College
Hill Thos, 1228 E Washington
Hill Mrs Ellen, ne cor 2d and Madison
Hill John, nw cor 9th and Carpenter
Hill C W, S 3d bet Scarritt and Allen
Hiller Edward, 321 N 6th

Hiller B, sw cor 8th and Mason
Hiller E, 113 N 6th, saloon
Hiller Fred, 821 S Spring
Hinton Jane, 809 E Adams
Hinder Fred, 1006 S Spring
Hinsey C C, 548 W Jefferson
Hinsley D, 1316 E Jackson
Hines Richard, 318 W Madison
Hinman Wm S, W Capitol av and Walnut
Hinshaw John, W Capitol av bet New and Walnut
Hickman Dr W A, over Diller's drug store
Hippler S, 99 (old number) W Wright
Hoge Miss Mattie, 118 E Mason
Hodge, 323 N 10th
Hoehn Wm, 416 E Monroe, barber
Hohn John, S 12th bet Clay and Kansas
Hohl Henry, 620 S 8th
Hoehn W, cor Wright and Spring
Hoff Henry, 920 922 924 E Washington
Hofferkamp John, S 3d bet Canedy and Scarritt
Hofferkamp & Bro, 618 E Monroe, livery
Hofferkamp Herman, 507 S 8th
Hofferkamp Geo, 621 E Monroe, bakery
Hofferkamp Geo, 421 S 8th
Hoffman Wm, W Mason w of Cox
Hoffman J, 320 S 4th, saloon
Hoffman Edward, 1035 S College
Hoffman Chas, 915 E Adams
Hoffman F P, 108 N 13th
Hoffman H D, 404 E Carpenter
Hoffman Philip, 1127 E Jefferson
Hoffman Geo, 805 E Miller
Hogans Mrs M, 822 E Miller
Homes Mrs M McKee, Bettie Stuart institute, cor 4th
    and Jackson
Hogan Mrs, 1603 E Adams
Hoglan Geo F, 1024 S 2d
Hoenmann C W, 922 S 4th
Holtman Lewis, 401 E Monroe
Holtman B, 415 S 11th
Holts Wm, 1522 E Capitol av
Holland Mrs Mary, 701 S 15th
Holland F, 726 E Reynolds
Hollem H B, W Monroe bet Lewis and New
Holly W H, E Monroe bet 7th and 8th, sale stable
Holly W H, S 7th bet Monroe and Capitol av
Holstein John, E Carpenter bet 1st and 2d
Howenstein Henry, 203 W Carpenter

Holzworth Fred, N 2d bet Madison and Mason
Hosel Joseph, ne cor Madison and 8th
Houswalt Michael, 220 W Cook
Hood Henry, Miller w of Rutlege
Hood Edward, 520 W Mason
Hoover A, E Jackson bet 12th and 13th
Hoole Geo, 1022 E Madison
Hood Wm, 218 S 4th
Hopkins Lee, 431 S New
Hopkins Jas A, N 7th bet Mason and Reynolds
Hopkins Mrs E A, 507 S College
Hopper John, S 2d bet Monroe and Capitol av, saloon.
Hopping D P, 216 E Monroe
Hoard Mrs Wm, ne cor Monroe and Lewis
Hohrein B, 302 W Reynolds
Horan Mrs, S Walnut bet Edwards and High
Horn Matthew, 1215 E Capitol av
Horn John, Mason bet 12th and 13th
Hoelscher Herman, 1128 N 1st
Horn Joseph, 830 E Madison
Horn J W, 17th and Moffatt av, n of Madison
Horn Samuel, N 8th bet Carpenter and Miller
Houchens G C, 1003 S 8th
Hostins Robt, 519 S 12th
Houck Mrs, 417 W Reynolds
House E P, 826 E Capitol av
Houseman Mollie, 333 E Washington bet 9th and 10th
Howard Timothy, 1013 E Madison
Howard Geo, 10th and N G av
Howard Geo, sw cor 13th and Carpenter
Howard Miss M, Jefferson bet 8th and 9th
Howard Wilson, sw cor Edwards and Spring
Howard John, 1211 E Jackson
Howe Jas, W Madison, w of Mill
Howell Martha E, 622 N 7th
Hoey Robt, 309 W Reynolds
Howey Preston, ne cor 7th and Mason, grocer
Howey Robt, 707 E Mason
Howey Thos, 1031 E Capitol av, grocer
Howey Chas, E Capitol av bet 9th and 10th
Hoag A S, ne cor Jefferson and Klein
Howarth Robt H, 1015 N 5th
Hook Martin, 11th s of S G av
Howett Henry, 10th and Cass
Hoyt C L, 621 N 6th
Hoyt J R, 720 E Mason
Hubart Mary, 1105 E Adams
Hugy R, 102 W Carpenter

Huber F, 114 W Mason
Hudson Frank, jr, 1050 N 5th
Hudson Mrs, E Capitol av bet 14th and 15th
Hudson Thos, 1411 E Adams
Hudson L A, 710 E Reynolds, newsman
Hudson J L, 1130 S 6th
Hudson Dennis, 403 N 15th
Hudson Gabel, Edwards and E G av
Huddleston Jas, Adams bet 17th and 18th
Huelsman F, 1401 E Edwards, grocer
Huckleberry Eli, 1425 E Washington
Hulit E, 728 S 11th
Hullihan Pat, 13th and Lincoln
Hughes John C, 914 W Washington
Hughes Dr, 313 W Monroe
Hughes Thos, Carpenter w end
Hunt John, 1813 E Capitol av
Hunt John, 523 S 11th
Hunt Mrs, E Adams
Hunt A, S 10th bet Jackson and Edwards
Hunter A N, 1st and N G av
Hunter Wm S, 811 S 4th
Huston Wm, ne cor 3d and Canedy
Huston L, 17th and Moffat
Hurley John, 1030 S 12th
Hurley Mrs Patrick, 1507 E Adams
Hurley Michael, W Jefferson, w of Mill
Hurst Morris, E Reynolds bet 1st and 2d
Hurer Joseph, se cor Rutlege and Calhoun av
Huttenhausen M, 903 S 12th
Hyde Mrs Erman, 809 E Adams
Hyde E B, S 7th bet Capitol av and Jackson
Hyde Wm, S 3d bet Washington and Adams

I DE A L, 305 nw cor 5th and Madison, foundry
Ide Henry, 1525 E Mason
Ide Ferd, 433 N 6th
Ihlenfeldt August, 428 W Washington
Ihlenfeldt Fred, 2d nr S G av
Ihlenfeldt Wm, 603 W Monroe
Immasche Henry, 915 S Pasfield
Ingram Mrs, cor 11th and Capitol av
Ingram Katie, Madison bet 11th and 12th
Ingram Gus, S 11th s of S G av
Irwin Mrs C C, 706 S 6th cor Cook
Irwin Robt, Madison bet 10th and 11th
Irwin Joseph, S 3d bet Scarritt and Allen

Irwin Washington, 1328 E Edwards
Irwin H C, 506 S 8th bet Jackson and Edwards
Ives H B, 610 W Monroe
Ives John G, 425 N 6th
Ives E R, 1101 E Monroe, grocery
Ives David S, 1217 E Monroe
Ives Ben, 744 W Jefferson

JACKSON A, 404 N 13th
    Jackson Mrs, 28 (old number) E Adams, laundry
    Jackson Geo, W Washington w of 1st
Jackson Boody, bet 15th and 16th
Jackson M Hitt, bet 15th and 16th
Jackson Chas, 119 W Wright
Jackson Walter, Miller bet 10th and 11th
Jackson Edward, 608 S 9th
Jackson J W H, 614 S 9th
Jackson Benjamin, 201 N 14th
Jacobs Adam, 1231 E Cook
Jacobs Chris, W Calhoun av
Jacobs Dan, 1702 E Capitol av
Jacoby Frank, 104 N 13th
Jacoby John, 10th and Barrett
Jagla Mrs Kate, Reynolds bet 8th and 9th
James Dr Lizzie P, 213 S 5th
James Frank, 220 W Allen
James W S, 1227 E Jackson
James Geo B, N 2d bet Carpenter and Union
James David, N 7th bet Bergen and N G av
Jamison Miss, Mason bet 9th and 10th
Jennings S A, 1111 E Adams
Jayne Dr Wm, 507 Enos av cor 5th
Jelley Matthew, 1155 N 7th
Jenkins J W, 1130 N 5th
Jenkins Eli A, nw cor 11th and Jefferson
Jenkins A, 86 (old number) N 4th and Mason
Jewel Thomas C, Madison bet 6th and 7th
Jewett Frank, S 9th bet Washington and Adams
Jewett Frank, 1817 E Adams
Joerger Mrs, 209 W Capitol av
Johan J, S 8th bet Clay and Scarritt
Job Jas, 410 N 5th
Joseph John, W Reynolds bet 1st and Klein
Johnson John, 905 S Spring
Johnson A, 14th and Adams e of 14th
Johnson P D, 1043 S 4th
Johnson Chas, 826 S 3d

Johnson Jas, 813 E Jefferson
Johnson Irwin, 1201 S 5th
Johnston R P, 427 N 4th
Johnson Jas, 120 W Carpenter
Johnson Thos N, 118 W Allen
Johnson John, 15th bet Madison and Mason
Johnston E S, 321 & 323 E Washington, Revere House
Johnson Willis, (over Withey's), machinist
Johnson Geo, 9th bet Washington and Jefferson
Johnson Jefferson, bet 10th and 11th
Johnson Thos, 719 E Washington
Johnson C T, 1177 N 4th
Johnston L E, 431 W Jefferson
Johnson Mrs, 323 N 7th
Johnson Geo W, 903 S 5th
Johnson Geo K, 230 W Edwards
Johnston John, N 2d bet Madison and Mason
Johnson Jas H, 1612 E Capitol av
Johnston Adam, 705 and 707 E Washington, marble
    works
Johnson Wm, 720 N 7th
Johnson John, 353 W Miller
Johnston John H, sw cor 2d and Charles
Johnston J A, 630 W Monroe
Johnson Jack, Reynolds bet 8th and 9th
Johnson J H, 630 S 9th
Johnson Wm T, 215 E Union
Johnston Robt, 1027 S 3d
Johnson Mrs, E Capitol av bet 15th and 16th
Jones Evan, 1116 E Washington
Jones Geo W, 503 S 7th
Jones Wm, S 3d bet Wright and Canedy
Jones Jas, S 6th bet Allen and Vine
Jones John A, 1015 S 6th
Jones Mrs Jane, S 8th bet Washington and Adams
Jones John T, 1028 E Jefferson
Jones Isaac, 1219 E Madison
Jones Frank, Mason bet 15th and 16th
Jones S H, 327 S 8th
Jones Mrs Annie, 216 N 9th
Jones Mrs, Miller bet 10th and 11th
Jones Richard, N 5th near N G av
Jones Eugene, cor 18th and Adams
Jones Frank, 15th n of Mason
Jones Lewis, 1423 E Monroe
Jones Mrs, 416 N 11th
Jones Thos, 13th bet Douglas and Cass
Jones Anderson, cor 10th and Monroe

Jones Mrs M J, S 3d bet Canedy and Scarritt
Jornes G W, 111½ ws square, Photographer
Judkins A B, 512 S W G av
Julian Jas, E Washington bet 9th and 10th
Justice J C, 1115 S 5th

KANE Rev A J, S 2nd bet Wright and Canedy
    Kane H B, 108 N 5th, J P
    Kain John 402 W Capitol av
Karvin Thos, 1109 E Washington
Kavanagh A G, 107 W Cook
Kavanagh Mrs C, 1031 S 6th
Kane Wm, 622 S Walnut
Karney Mrs Mary, 626 S Walnut
Karn Geo, 1125 S 12th
Kaufman Chas P, 102 W Cook
Kerns A K, 125 N 6th, grocer
Keazer Reuben, 219 W Edwards
Keedy John D, 1003 S 4th
Keefer Samuel, 226 W Cook
Keefner Jennie, ne cor 7th and Adams
Keefner John, nw cor 1st and Reynolds
Keenan M, 13th and Adams
Keiley T J, sw cor 5th and N G av, grocer
Kelchner W W, 1016 S 4th
Keller J K, 402 S 5th
Kelly Daniel, 840 S Spring, saloon
Kelly James, 217 W Mason
Kelley Andrew, 604 N 7th
Kelley Mrs, N 7th bet Carpenter and Miller
Kelley W F, 218 N 2d
Kelley Wm, 612 E Adams, up stairs
Kelley John, 210 N 4th
Kelley Henry, 1015 E Washington
Kelly J J, 700 and 702 E Washington, Jefferson House
Kelly Henry, sr, ne cor 2d and Allen
Kelher C, 224 W Mason
Kelsey Isaac, Carpenter bet 11th and 12th
Keeling Squire, 709 S 15th
Kendall Mrs, 1004 E Mason
Kennedy Jas A, 110 N 6th, attorney
Kennedy F P, 520 E Monroe, saloon
Kennedy Jas, 822 E Washington, horse shoeing
Kennedy Mrs F, 728 E Jefferson
Kennedy Chas, se cor 5th and Elm
Kennedy   , 831 E Mason
Kennedy Thos F, 821 E Washington, horse shoeing

Kennedy Patrick, 534 W Williams ·
Kennedy M, 621 W Herndon
Kennedy Thos F, 1119 E Jefferson
Kennedy M, Madison bet 10th and 11th
Kent Richard, Edwards bet 15th and 16th
Kenneth Edward, 2201 W Reynolds
Kent Jessie, 908 E Miller
Kenyon Geo, 828 E Miller
Kern A, sw cor 7th and Miller
Kerns A K, 9th bet Enos av and Lincoln
Kernes Robt, ne cor Madison and 8th
Kerlin Micheal, Mill and Jefferson
Kerns Patrick, 308 W Carpenter
Kern Chris, ne cor 8th and Adams
Kernohan Samuel, 843 S 3d
Kerr S C, 1217 E Capitol av
Kerch Julius, W Mason bet Rutlege and Cox
Kervin Patrick, 313 W Madison
Kerr Benjamin, 411 W Jefferson
Kessberger A, 1st bet Washington and Jefferson
Kessler A, 52 W Reynolds ´
Kettler C H, 214 N 2nd
Ketcher John, 1003 S 11th
Ketcher Wm, 713 S Eleventh
Keydell Mrs, Carpenter W E
Kepner John, 604 W Washington
Keyes Mrs, 1820 E Washington
Keyes Isaac, 527 S 7th
Keyes Jas W, 714 W Washington
Keyes Chas A, N 6th bet Elm and Enos av
Keyes Wm, S 10th bet Capitol av and Jackson
Kidd T W S, 422 S 8th
Kidd C P, 229 N 5th
Kilner Dr, 406 E Adams
Kiley Pat, N 8th bet Miller and Enos av
Kiley Mrs C, 1128 N 4th
Killskie John, 542 W Jefferson
Killion Mrs, 1312 E Washington
Killgallon Michael, 928 E Miller
Killion Thos, 1818 E Adams
Killius Fred, sw cor 8th and Jackson
Kimber Gus A, 914 S 2d
Kimber W F, 521 S 6th
Kimble P F, 1004 S 6th
Kibber A, 1117 S 11th
King Henry, S 18th bet Monroe and Capitol av
King W D, E Adams bet 12th and 13th
King Annie, 222 N 8th
    —9

King Henry 215 W Capitol av
King J LaF, 425 E Jefferson, up stairs, tar drops
King J R H, 215 S 6th, attorney
King Thos. E Carpenter bet 2d and 3d
King W J, 1102 E Capitol av
Kingdon John, 309 E Carpenter
Kinney Thos, 1106 E Adams
Kinney John, 1113 N 9th
Kinsler Jas, 1608 E Washington
King J, 301 E Jefferson, Germania House
Kinsler Michael, 924 S Spring
Kienchler M, 1017 N 4th
Kienchler Jacob, 1032 E Rafter
Kinney Thos, 1804 E Washington
Kinable, ne cor 3d and Wright
Kirst John, 909 S 11th, grocer
Kiser A, 1318 E Capitol av
Kizer W H, 1005 S 11th
Kirch Mrs B, 1032 Rafter bet 3d and 4th
Klein Wm, Madison bet 8th and 9th
Klein A, Madison bet 8th and 9th
Klein Henry A, 1404 E Edwards
Klintworth Dedrick, 1415 E Edwards
Klock Mrs E, 529 N 11th
Kluessner A, 410 W Carpenter
Knapp Mrs A L, 725 S 6th
Knapp Fred, 1006 E Miller
Knopel M, 832 S 2d
Knople Joseph, cor 13th and Capitol av
Knotts A H, 818 S 13th
Knox Mrs Mary, 1505 E Jackson
Knox Thos, 1330 E Adams
Knoder Wm, 852 N 1st
Koch Casper, ne cor Carpenter and Klein
Koch Mrs, 406 W Carpenter
Koop N A, 1426 E Adams
Koch Adam, 411 W Carpenter
Koesber A, 913 S Spring
Koester A, 914 S Spring, shoe shop
Kochendorfer M, 10th bet Jackson and Edwards
Kohlbruck John, 462 W Carpenter
Kramaer M, 931 E Cook, saloon
Kramaer Mrs, cor 15th and Cook
Kramaer Jacob, cor 14th and Douglas
Kramer John, S 9th bet Edwards and Cook
Kramaer B, 626 S 9th
Kray Geo, S 15th bet Cook and Douglas
Krenzkemper H, 413 E Adams, bakery
Kramp N, 1524 E Edwards

Kriegh Eli M, 518 W Monroe
Keigan John, 326 W Reynolds
Kriegh Eli, 644 N 5th
Kreider Dr, 313 S 6th
Kriegh Mrs Mary, 214 W Reynolds
Krodell Geo W, 1100 E Jefferson
Kroel Chas, 1054 N Rutlege
Krueger Wm, 219 S 6th, confectionery
Kruger Henry, 309 W Cook
Kruse John C, 102 E Cook
Kroz Jacob, 1013 E Carpenter
Kraus Mrs Margaret, 846 S 2d
Kuecher Wm, 1319 E Monroe
Kuecher John, 702 S 12th
Kuehn J, 727 E Reynolds
Kuehn A, 312 W Wright
Koehn Chas, 301 W Cook
Kun Fred, 208 S 5th, saloon
Kunz Adam 313 N 5th
Kunzweiler & Knoppel 609 E Washington, bakery
Kusel 502 N 5th
Kusel & Co, 205 S 5th, clothing
Kusel J, ne cor 6th and Washington, clothing
Kussmaul Wm F, 931 S 11th, grocer
Kurran Chas, 222 W Edwards
Kurbey Chas, 406 W Williams
Kirkendall John N, se cor 9th and Adams

LARRABEE REV E A, 312 E Adams
  Labarthe Julius, 623 E Adams
    LaBonte M, 531 N 5th
Lacey John, 1513 E Washington
Lacer Mrs, 927 E Cook
Lahey James,1001 S 14th
Lake Thos, 705 N 3d
Lakin A A, S 1st bet Allen and Vine
Lamb John C, 408 W Monroe
Lamb Mrs Jas L, 206 E Adams
Lamkin Frank, 933 S College
Landauer Mrs, N 7th bet Madison and Mason
Langan Jacob, S 14th and Cass
Lange B A, 626 N 6th
Landering Joseph, 606 W Hay
Lanahan Edward, se cor Canedy and 2nd
Lanahan Mrs, 908 E Carpenter
Lanphier C H, 325 N 4th
Lanphier John C, nw cor 6th and Miller
Larbaur John, 535 W Canedy

Larkin Wm, 18th and Monroe
Larsch O T, 1320 E Adams
Lasswell Moses, 831 S Spring
Lasswell Mrs V B, 321 W Capitol av
Late A. Mason bet 11th and 12th
Latham Dr A, 223 S 5th, dentist
Latham A R, 101 N Doyle av
Latham Geo, 1304 E Monroe
Latham H C, 1203 S 6th
Latham Mrs P C, 401 S 7th
Latham A, 216 W Edwards
Latham & Souther, 221 S 6th, abstract office
Lathrop Richard, S 9th bet Edwards and Cook
Lauterbach Peter, Elliot av bet Bond and Walnut
Lauterbach Mrs M, 1126 S 11th
Langerman W, S 4th bet Vine and S G av
Lauer Henry, 343 W Miller
Laughlin F D, 122 N 6th, dentist
Lavenworth L F, 616 S 7th
Lavely Wm M, 1049 N 5th
Lavely Wm, 1007 N 5th
Lawler John A, 616 S 8th
Lawler Mrs, 1326 E Adams
Lawler Thos, 828 E Monroe
Lawler Wm, S 8th bet Scarritt and Allen
Lawler John, 130 E Jefferson, feed store
Lawless Wm S, 1133 N 9th
Lawrence R D, 727 S 4th
Lawrence Frank, 1101 S 12th
Lawrence Mrs, 819 E Carpenter
Lawrence R D, office 227 S 6th
Layman Jesse, N 5th bet Jefferson and Madison, Ohio
    House
Leitz Lewis A, 718 S 12th
Leech R C, S 8th bet Cook and Douglas
Leaf Wm, S 8th bet Edwards and Cook
Leary Thos, 1230 E Washington, grocer
Leck Herman, 305 W Jackson
Leber Joseph, 522 N 7th
Leber Edward, 507 W Reynolds
Leddy Thos, 1110 N 7th
LeClair Mrs N, 1489 E Jackson
Ledgerwood N G, 9th and Enterprise
Lee John S, Adams bet 14th and 15th
Lee Geo, W Carpenter W of 322
Lee Miss Mattie, 216 S 8th
Lee Maggie, N 10th bet Reynolds and Carpenter
Lee Thos, S 5th bet Edwards and Cook
Lee N D, S 6th bet Scarritt and Allen

Lee Edward W, ne cor W Capitol av and Walnut
Lee Peter, 1225 E Adams
Lee Jessie, cor 10th and Carpenter
Leese Mrs, E Jefferson bet 10th and 11th
Leeder Wm, 1026 S Spring
Leeder Henry, 1012 S Spring
Leggott Geo, 700 S 5th
Leggott A, 712 S 5th
LeGrand G W, 228 W Allen
LeGrand Robt, 11th S of Cass
LeGrand Williamson 1044 S Spring
Leigh Wm, N 1st S of N G av
Leland Hotel, nw cor 6th and Capitol av
Leutenmeyer Chas, 222 E Jefferson
Leutenmeyer Joseph, N 8th bet Divison and N G av
Lenters J P, E Cook bet 12th and 13th
Leonard Thos, 1113 E Washington
Lenox Albert, 82 (old number) N 4th and Mason
Leroy Miss C, 404 E Adams, hair goods
Leroy N, 404 E Adams, machinist
Leutenmeyer Max, 525 W Reynolds
Lumis Wm, Reynolds bet 11th and 12th
Leitner Geo, ne cor 8th and Cook
Leterle B, 915 E Reynolds
Levi Mrs, 324 N 5th
Levi Z, 500 N 5th
Lewis Geo, 409 E   onroe, up stairs
Lewis Mrs Tinnie, 300 N 15th
Lewis Wm, 406 S Doyle av
Lewis A P, 319 W Cook
Lewis Reuben, 229 N 2d
Lewis Henry, 619 E Miller
Lewis Obed, 423 S 6th
Lewis Mrs Martha, E G av and Edwards
Lewis Benjamin, nw cor 2d and Madison
Lewis John, 914 E Madison
Lewis W, 605 W Edwards
Lewis John, Mason bet 15th and 16th
Liddy M, W Mason bet 1st and Klein
Lilley W H, S 4th bet Adams and Monroe, tin shop
Lilley Wm, W Washington and John
Lindley U, 629 W Jefferson
Lindsay Isaac, 102 W Scarritt
Lindsay Dr V T, 608 S 5th
Livenger Adam, S Spring bet Allen and Vine
Lick Fred, 430 W Canedy
Link Val, 330 W Mason
Link Val & Bro, 425 E Washington, saloon
Link L, 346 W Carpenter

Little G J, 131 S 2d
Little S N & Son, nw cor 4th and Adams, livery stable
Littler D T, nw cor Miller and Klein
Lloyd R, nw cor 3d and Madison
Lloyd T W, 917 S 5th
Lochner Rev Fred, E Jefferson bet 1st and 2d
Lochmiller Thos, 311 W Miller
Loeb Henry, N Rutledge N of Miller
Loeb Wm, Miller bet 1st and 2d
Lopes Joseph, Monroe bet 8th and 9th
Loeb Adam, 331 W Miller, wagon shop and blacksmith
Loeser Frank, 214 N 5th, saloon
Lofy Nicholas, 818 S 12th
Logan Mrs Jennie, nw cor 9th and Monroe
Logan Wm, 1331 E Cook
Logan L, se cor Miller and 8th
Logan Henry H, 1323 E Cook
Logan Jas, 1535 E Mason
Loggie Jas, State bet Washington and Adams
Loahman Mrs, W Mason W of Cox
Lanergan John, se cor Miller and Klein
Long Jerry, 1205 E Monroe
Long Chas H, 215 S 5th, bakery and confectionery
Longnecker Wm, Jefferson bet 8th and 9th, saloon
Loomis Wm E, 427 E Washington, attorney
Loomis Geo, 927 E Cook
Loomis H, 221 E Jackson
Lord Mrs Dr, 200 E Washington
Lord Dr J J, 609 W Jefferson
Lorsch Chas, 320 N 5th
Lott Jas A, 310 W Cook
Love Thos, E Jefferson bet 3d and 4th, saloon
Lowery Thos, 1304 E Adams
Lowry John B, cor 15th and Capitol av
Luby Thos, 608 S 11th
Luce Mrs, 1115 E Adams
Lumis Flora, 208 N 14th
Lucky Lewis, 718 N 6th
Lumpp A, 521 S 9th
Lund T, 823 E Adams
Lundahl B B, 121 N 6th
Lusk D W, 927 S 8th
Luttrell Theo, 10;9 N 5th
Lutricks John, 1100 S 11th
Lutz John M, N Klein bet Mason and Reynolds cooper
    shop)
Lutz John, 421 W Reynolds
Lynch Michael, Washington bet 15th and 16th
Lynch Henry, 1124 E Madison

Lynch Michael, 1726 E Mason
Lynch M, 17th and Adams
Lynch C W, 550 W William
Lyden Michael, 15th and Jefferson
Lyer Nick, west end of Carpenter
Lyons Burt, 835 S 3d

MAAK MRS MARY, 313 W Edwards
Mackey W, 324 W Adams
Mack R E, 511 ns square, Boston shoe store
Mace M, 1103 S 8th
Mack M, 919 E Cook
Mackbey Miss, 1407 E Edwards
Madison Jas, Adams e of 16th
Maggenti Joseph, 624 W Monroe
Maggenti Louis, 624 W Monroe
Maher P, 621 E Adams, grocer
Maher Patrick, 713 E Adams
Maher John, 326 W Reynolds
Maher M, 302 N 13th
Mahn Mrs T, 823 E Carpenter
Maheney M, N 8th bet Division and N G av
Mahan P, 618 E Adams
Mahon Michael, Elliott av
Mahoney Dan, 1206 E Adams
Mahoney Dennis, N 7th n of Bergen
Mahoney Wm, 14th and E Monroe
Mahoney Michael, 800 S 14th
Mahoney P, 446 W Carpenter
Mahoney Tim, cor 11th and Jackson
Mahoney Wm, 926 S 12th
Mahoney Jerry, 1009 S 3d
Mahoney John, 435 W Reynolds
Mahoney John, 1024 S 11th
Mahoney John, W Jefferson and John
Mahoney John, N 7th N of Bergen
Maloney Mrs, 1609 E Adams
Maloney Wm, 1605 E Adams, city marshal
Maloney Ed, 625 E Wsshington, up stairs
Maloney Thos, cor 13th and Cass
Mallory R V, 524 N 6th
Maloney Pat, E Washington bet 1st and 2d
Maldon J C, E Capitol av bet 9th and 10th
Malone Mrs M, 9th bet Washington and Jefferson
Maltner E, Madison bet 9th and 10th
Malter Jacob, 229 E Carpenter
Mallette Mrs, 1130 S 7th
Mallory Mrs Nora, 211 S Doyle av

Maisel Mrs A, 825 E Reynolds
Maisenbecker M, 1228 E Capitol av
Maisenberger Geo, 2127 E Madison
Maisenback Fritz, N 8th bet Division and N G av
Mambach Wm, 809 E Madison
Monahan Hugh, 302 W Carpenter
Mann Geo W, se cor 11th and Capitol av
Mann Geo B, 402 sw cor Monroe ond Pasfield
Mars A B, 717 E Mason
Marx John, 1003 S 11th
Markey Patrick, 1709 E Adams
Marker John, 1025 E Jefferson
Markham David, 116 (old number) N 5th
Marsh Henry S, 417 S 11th
Marshall S H, cor 7th and Adams, Marshall House
Marshall John, 1119 N Rutlege
Martin Mrs Ellen, 231 N 1st
Martin Samuel, 319 W Edwards
Martin Joseph, 1403 E Adams
Martin Isaac, 319 W Wright
Martin Toney, Adams bet 14th and 15th
Martin J V, 831 E Madison
Marz Lewis, 932 W Jefferson
Marks Jacob, 1015 S 12th
Mason Thos, Reynolds bet 7th and 8th
Mason N, 909 N 6th
Matheny Mrs C W, 813 S 6th
Matheny C O, S 5th bet Wright and Canedy
Matheny E D, W G av bet Monroe and Washington
Matheny Cook, sw cor Monroe and Doyle av
Matheny Mrs N W, 825 S 6th
Matheny C O, office 221 S 6th
Matheny Hon J H, se cor 6th and Scarritt
Matheny J H, jr, office 102 S 6th
Mather T S, 106 N 5th, real estate agent
Mather Thos C, ne cor Walnut and High
Matthews Jas, 415 W Capitol av
Matter Wm, E Edwards bet 16th and 17th
Matthews J, 1116 E Mason
Matthews Mrs C, se cor Edwards and Spring
Matthews Mrs Ruth N 2nd bet Carpenter and Union
Mathies Lenord, 100 W Reynolds
Mathies Valentine, S 10th bet Capitol av and Jackson
Maurer Chas, se cor 11th and Edwards
Maurer M, 211 W Mason, grocer and saloon
Maurer Chas, 917 E Washington, liquor store
Mau Mrs Mary, 309 W Washington
Maxcy Jas R, 1119 S 4th
Maxcy Jas R, 501 E Washington, jeweler

Maxcy Joseph, 622 N 2nd
Maxcy J C, nw cor 3d and Madison
Maxfield A J, 909 E Miller
Maxmillion Philip, 904 E Reynolds
Maxwell R W, 720 S 5th
Maxwell R W, 517 ns Square
Maxwell Wm, 1131 E Jackson
Maxwell Wm R, 704 S 7th
Maxon Mrs, 112 E Reynolds
May Miss E, 10th bet Madison and Mason
Mayhew Wm, 1021 S College
Mayol Chas, 1024 E Madison
Mayol M, 136 N 13th
Mayol F, 212 N 14th
Mayol M, 414 E Adams, tailor shop
Myers F, 330 N 6th
McBride Chas, 400 W Adams
McBurnie Dr W S, 203 E Adams
McBurnie Dr, office Leland Hotel
McCabe Wm, 610 N 8th
McCabe Wm, 207 E Adams
McCabe Mrs, sw cor Spring & Monroe, boarding house
McCaffery John, 1037 N Rutlege
McCague Wm, 626 S 6th
McCaffery John, 915 N 1st
McCammely David, Madison bet 7th and 8th
McCann Moses, N 5th bet Rafter and N G av
McCarthy Fred, 1102 E Capitol av
McCartney Jas, 105 W Monroe
McCarty John, Miller bet 10th and 11th
McCarty Dennis, 1614 E Washington
McCarty Mrs Anne, W Hay
McCarty Jerry, 625 W Hay
McCarty T, E Capitol av bet 14th and 15th
McCarty L, 17th and Monroe
McCarty Wm, 1125 E Adams
McCarty John, 1127 E Adams
McCarty Mrs Anne, 901 S 11th
McCarty J, nw cor Carpenter and Rutlege
McCarty Jerry, nw cor of Hay and Bond
McCarty Pat, N 8th bet Division and N G av
McCauley A E, Jefferson bet 4th and 5th, blacksmith
McLean John, 1211 E Adams
McLean Mrs A S, N 6th bet Reynolds and Carpenter
McLean P H, 1226 E Mason
McClennan Daniel, 121 N 14th
NcClellan B, 210 N 14th
McClernand & Keyes, 101 ws Square, attorneys
—10

McClernand J A, 529 6th and Enos av
McCauley A, 120 E Carpenter
McCullough Edward, cor 6th and N G av
McConnell Edward, 113 W Cook
McConnell John, 516 ss Square, insurance
McConnell R S, 1007 S College
McCormick John, 1108 E Adams
McCormick John, 13th bet Reynolds and Carpenter
McCormick Samuel, 1402 E Washington
McCormick John, 1408 E Jackson
McCormick A R, 525 Monroe
McCormick Mrs Anne, N 8th bet Miller and Enos av
McCormick Thos, S Spring bet Wright and Canedy
McCormick D N, sw cor 2d and Carpenter
McCoy Michael, 108 W Jefferson
McCosker A, nw cor 6th and Edwards
McCreery John, St Nicholas Hotel 4th and Jefferson
McCue Neil, N 14th bet Jefferson and Madison
McCutcheon Geo, 1329 E Adams, grocery
McDowell C, 422 Walnut
McDaniel Gilbert, 1601 E Cook
McDonnald Daniel, 634 W Calhoun av
McDonnald Mrs, 1212 E Washington
McDonnald S, sw cor 10th and Mason
McDonnald, 118 W Wright
McDonnald John 1503 E Adams
McDonnald J H, 1035 S College
McElhiney Mrs M, 610 S 5th
McElowe Mrs Ellen, cor 10th and Cook
McEuen Theodore, 912 E Mason, ticket agt
McGravey Jas, 1106 E Adams
McEwen J H, N 12th bet Miller and Enos av
McGinnis John, 14th bet Jefferson and Madison
McGinnis Jas, N Bond
McGovern John, 1718 E Washington
McGovery Mrs, 1030 E Washington
McGowan Edward, cor 11th and N G av
McGowen Michael, 429 S New
McGrath Thos, 1213 E Washington
McGraw John, 322 W Carpenter
McGraw Mrs, W Jefferson w of Mill
McGraw T C, 1122 E Washington
McGraw J Adams, cor 4th and Madison, grocer
McGraw Mrs, 308 N 13th
McGraw Mrs, 124 N 13th
McGraw Dan, 14th bet Cass and Clay
McGuire B, 212 N 4th
McGrue Thos, 1218 S 7th
McGuire R L, 630 N 6th

McGuire Thos, 830 E Carpenter
McGuire, Hamilton & Salzenstein, 215 S 6th
McGuirk John, 1519 E Adams
McNerney John, cor 14th and Cook
McInnes Mrs M E, 517 E Jefferson, dress maker
McIrney James, sw cor 12th and Mason
McIntire Mrs, 219 W Jefferson
McKee Mrs M, 14th n of Mason
McKee Robt, 514 N 4th
McKee J C, 1426 E Capitol av
McKee Geo, 1213 E Washington
McKee Kate, 415 E Monroe
McKelvey Hugh, Miller bet 9th and 10th
McKernan Patrick, N Elliott av
McKinzie Geo, 1026 E Reynolds
McKinzie Joseph, 1208 E Mason
McLaughlin Jane, 308 W Carpenter
McMahon Jas, 933 S 5th
McMichael E S, se cor 8th and Division
McMahon Jas, 224 E Washington
McManus Mrs E, 1116 N 7th
McManus Thos, 1602 E Washington
McNamara M, 526 W Mason
McNamara Mrs Jane, 827 E Adams
McMurphy Lester, ne cor 3d and Allen
McNamara John, 309 E Madison
McNamara Patrick, 1017 S 13th
McNamara M, 1712 E Adams
McNulty F, 504 ss Square, city gallery
McQuin W F, 429 W Edwards
McSherry Patrick, 1405 E Monroe
McVeigh Luther, cor Cook and Douglas
McFall Wm, 802 S 12th
McFarland W A, 814 E Carpenter
McGurty Hugh, 806 S College
McCurley S D, cor 18th and Cook
McCullough John, 403 N 5th
McGready John, N 2d bet Madison and Mason
McNiel J F, 200 S Walnut
McRoberts John, se cor 4th and Cook
Meisenbacher J, 100 W Mason, grocery & saloon
Meissner Prof. B, 321 S 5th, music teacher
Meschler Philip, cor 8th and Edwards
Melcher Wm, 817 S College
Meldrum Jas, 1308 E Monroe
Meyerhoff Henry L, 610 N 7th
Mellin N J, 220 N 2d
Melcher W M, 420 E Monroe, tailor shop
Melton & Logan, 220 N 7th, farm machinery

Melton J C, 915 E Mason
Mendonsa M, 931 Mason
Mondonsa Mrs Mary, 211 E Carpenter
Mendell John, 817 E Madison
Mendell Geo S, 410 S 5th
Mendell John, ne cor 11th and Madison
Menchini John, 407 E Monroe, confectionery
Mench Mrs, W Washington w of gas works
Merkle Adam H, 106 E Madison
Merkle Herman, nw cor Cook and Spring, meat market
Merklin Jacob, Herndon opp. Reisch's brewery
Merklin L, 207 S 5th, bakery & confectionery
Merklin H, nw cor Rutlege and Calhoun av
Merklin Lambert, W Capitol av cor Lewis
Merryman W J, 903 S 2d
Merrick John, 622 W Monroe
Merritt E L, 231 W Capitol av
Metz Geo V, W Reynolds
Metzger Geo, cor 11th and Adams, meat market
Metzger Geo, 926 N 3d
Metzger Wm, 401 E Monroe, meat market
Metzger Wm, N Rutlege, opposite brewery
Metzger Geo, 516 E Monroe, meat market
Metzger A, W Adams, bet Spring and College
Mette Fred, 101 E Wright
Metcher Mrs R, 107 E Reynolds
Meyer Geo, 613 E Washington, shoe shop
Meyer John, 207 W Mason
Midden Henry, ne cor Cook and Spring, grocer
Mickey Nelson, 205 E Carpenter
Michael Richard, 227 S 5th, dry goods
Michow F, reservoir
Miller Gus, 13th bet Cook and Douglas
Miller Mrs Henry, 914 N 1st
Miller Wm B, 103 S 5th, hardware
Miller Henry, 522 S 11th
Miller J P H, 726 N 7th
Miller John, 205 E Carpenter
Miller Mary, S Walnut and Canedy
Miller Wm B, 829 S 2d
Miller Wm, 422 W Adams
Miller Thomas, 880 S 13th
Miller Mrs S, 114 S 9th
Miller Jacob H, N 3d bet Union and Rafter
Miller Thomas, Carpenter bet 8th and 9th
Miller Wm, nw cor 7th and Miller
Miller W C, 1123 E Washington
Miller Pat, cor 18th and Cook
Miller Jacob, N State bet Washington and Jefferson

Miller Annie, 1200 E Monroe
Miller Otto, 13th bet Cook and Douglas
Million Dr J L, 516 S 6th
Million Dr Edward A, office Million's block
Mills Mrs M, 908 S College
Mills Thomas, 317 N 11th
Milton William, 1211 E Adams
Minard Mrs, 1022 E Mason
Minard Warren, 308 N 10th
Miner Mrs O H, 405 S 5th .
Mischler Phillip, E Edwards bet 9th and 10th
Misterly John W, Herndon w of Rutlege
Mitchell Charles, se cor High and W G av
Mitchell Wm, 411 N 4th
Mirkle A, 305 N 14th
Mirkle F X; 613, N 4th
Mockler Mrs M, 912 N 6th
Mockler Jas, S 4th, bet Monroe and Capitol av
Mohr A, 904 E Monroe
Moss Frank, 1031 E Miller
Moses John, 230 W Monroe
Monahan Mrs, 1002 S Spring
Monnett Jacob, N 7thn n of Bergen
Monnett Miss Mary, N 7th bet Bergen and N G av
Monnett Maggie, 12th bet Mason and Reynolds
Montague Eva, 68 E Mason bet 10th and 11th
Monitor office 615 E Monroe, opposite P O
Montgomery Hugh, 936 S 5th
Montgomery Wm M, 1501 E Washington
Moon R H, 416 W Monroe
Mooney James, 1721 E Adams
Mooney S P, 331 S 5th
Moore Lewis, 929 E Edwards
Moore Mrs M, S 8th, bet Cook and Douglas
Moore Wm H, 218 S 5th, book publisher
Moody Charles, 720 S 4th
Modley A E, Miller bet 9th and 10th
Moldiner John, 1316 E Capitol av
Molton David, 919 S 13th
Money L A, 1202 E Adams
Moore Alford A, 1108 E Reynolds
Moore A E & Co, S 8th bet Edwards and Cook, grocers
Moore A, 726 S 15th
Moore A, cor 15th and Jefferson
Moore & Clayton, 409 E Monroe, grocers
Morowski Charles, 437 N 6th
Moody & Crabb, 130 N 6th, dry goods
Morehead J C, 1210 S 5th
Morehead —, State bet Washington and Adams

Moran Mrs Dr, 227 S 7th
Morgan William, 730 N 8th
Morgan C M, 112 W Monroe
Morgan L, Mason bet 15th and 16th
Morgan H, 527 S 9th
Morgan Dr G W, 314 S 7th
Morney A, 1214 E Adams
Morris A W, W Grand Av bet Wash'n and Jefferson
Morris Joseph, 1411 E Capitol av
Morris H, 1105 E Capitol av
Morris A, 405 S 9th
Morris James, 409 S 11th
Morris M, 902 E Madison
Morse Mrs N, 220 E Monroe
Morse J M, 822 E Capitol av
Morse J. W, Mason bet 11th and 12th
Morton Annie, N 9th bet Madison and Mason
Motley David, N 8th bet Bergen and N Gr av
Mowery Joseph, 100 S Madison
Mowery Henry, E Edwards bet 16th and 17th
Mowery John H, S 8th bet Edwards and Cook
Mowery Edward, 117 W Carpenter
Mowery A, N 1st bet Pine and Hay
Mowery Gus, N 1st bet Pine and Hay
Mueller H E, 130 N 6th liquor store
Mueller G A, 226 S 5th liquors and cigars
Mueller G A, 700 E Reynolds
Mueller Chas, 127 N 5th, saloon
Mueller H, 410 S Walnut
Muller Alexander, 623 N 8th
Muldoon B, 112 N 6th, saloon
Muldoon James, 1303 E Edwards
Muldoon Mrs, 1303 E Edwards
Mulligan James, 922 E Miller
Mullin John 708 E Madison
Mullin Mrs, 1202 E Washington
Mullin Richard, 1120 E Reynolds
Mullen William, 230 W Cook
Mullin Mrs E, sw cor 12th and Reynolds
Mullen Mrs Sarah, 1519 E Adams
Mulquin Patrick, 831 S 3d
Mulready John, 1508 E Washington
Mulvey C, 1103 N Rutledge
Mulvey Patrick, N 7th, bet Carpenter and Miller
Murphy Mrs, 1023 E Washington
Murphy Patrick, 525 S 11th
Murphy Thos, 548 W Washington
Murphy Mrs Anne, W Miller west end
Murphy J G, 231 S 3d, hat Bleachery

Murphy Jas S, 416 E Washington, grocer
Murphy Peter, E Monroe bet 8th and 9th
Murphy Peter, S 11th s of Cass
Murphy John, 11th s of Clay
Murphy John, 443 W Reynolds
Murphy Mrs, 1101 S 12th
Murphy Jas, cor 12th and Jackson
Murrya Jas, 1228 E Jackson ·
Murray Mrs B, 524 WWilliams
Murraay C, 118 & 120 N 5th, restaurant
Murray Chas, 1109 E Washington
Murray Jas, Madison bet 10th and 11th
Murray Michael, Madison bet 12th and 13th
Murray G W, 216 N 2d
Murray Mrs T, 1628 E Washington,
Murry & Turner, 425 E Washington, attornies
Mussillon Joseph, 1108 E Jefferson
Mursinnc, 717 E Carpenter
Muttera H W, Reynolds e of 347
Muttera H, 418 E Washington, saloon
Myers J D, S 7th bet Edwards and Cook
Myers Adam, nw cor 9th and Miller
Myers Mrs Margaret, 6th and N G av
Myers Mrs Henry, 518 S 9th
Myers Frank, 518 S 9th
Myers Mrs C R, 114 S 9th
Myer Geo, 813 E Miller
Myers Mrs, cor 12th and Douglas
Myers Henry, 1008 E Monroe
Myers John, 1414 E Monroe
Myers Henry, 1320 E Monroe
Myers Mrs C, 801 E Jefferson
Myers Mrs Kate, 801 E Reynolds
Myers Manuel, 301 N 6th
Myers Pat, 1142 N 5th
Myers Michael, 1000 E Jefferson, saloon
Myers Frank, 513 us Square, wonder store
Myers, Davidson & Henley, ne cor 6th and Jefferson,
  wagon & carriage shop

NAFEW JOHN A, 425 E Jefferson
  Nagel & Diehr, 230 W Mason, grocers
  Nailor Abner, 919 E Carpenter
Nash Mrs, Washington bet 16th and 17th
Nash Emma, N 9th bet Jefferson and Madison
Naylor J W, 1017 E Carpenter
Neil John, 723 E Carpenter
Neal Wm, ne cor 6th and Monroe, barber shop

Neef Matthew, 417 E Washington, saloon
Neef M E, 1227 E Washington
Neef E, 509 E Monroe, liquor store
Neef A T, E Cook bet 1st and 2d
Neef Jacob, 315 W Carpenter
Neef Mrs, N 12th bet Reynolds and Carpenter
Neef Geo, 429 N 2d
Neef John, 1123 N 3d
Nees Dennis, 231 N 5th, grocer
Nehr Judson, S 7th bet Vine and S G av
Nehr Nelson, 1017 S 8th
Neilson A, 113 N 5th, saloon
Nelch Henry, N 12th bet Reynolds and Carpenter
Nelch John, 520 N 12th
Nelch Adam, 506 N 4th
Nealon Patrick, ne cor 5th and Scarritt
Nelson John, S 7th bet Washington and Adams
Nelson John, 631 E Adams, saloon
Nelson Geo, N 6th s of N G av
Nelson Wm, 15th and Jefferson
Nelson O K, 120 E Madison
Nelson Chas, 909 E Carpenter
Nelson Wm, W Canedy bet Walnut and Henrietta
New Mrs Addie, 1224 E Edwards
Neu Jacob, 1027 E Carpenter
Neu Cris, 1029 E Carpenter
Newland Mrs Sarah, 1011 E Adams
Newman John, W Carpenter bet 6th and 7th
Newman N, 224 S 5th, restaurant
Newman N, S 6th bet Monroe and Capitol av
Newman Wm, 5th and Jefferson, up stairs
Newman J C, 414 W Adams
Newman H F, 326 W Edwards
Newman Fred, 316 W Edwards
Newton Robt, cor 18th and Douglas
Newquist Chas, S 12th and Clay
Nichols Mrs, 526 S 7th
Nicholas A, cor 18th and Edwards
Nicholas John H, 1228 E Adams
Nicholson Daniel, sw cor 2d and Madison
Niesen Wm, 730 S College
Niles Lotus, 414 S 8th
Nichols Wm, 1019 S 4th
Noell Moses, 1123 E Madison
Noland John, Adams e of 10th
Nolan Patrick, 224 W Jefferson, grocer
Norman A D, 931 S 5th
Norris John, 925 E Cook
North A A, 618 E Mason

Nonenmann Jacob, 610 S 7th
Nuckols J M, sw cor Washington and Walnut
Nunes Wm, 410 N 14th
Nunes Joseph, cor 13th and Clay
Nunis John, 1123 N 6th
Nurse Samuel, N 9th bet Division and N G av
Nuess Henry, E Edwards bet 8th and 9th
Nusbaum Benjamin, 528 N 5th
Nutt Isaac, 118 E Reynolds

O'BOYLE PATRICK, 1023 E Washington
O'Brien Wm, 401 W Mason
O'Brien Dennis, 131 W Mason
O'Brien Mrs, 828 E Madison
O'Brien T, 14th bet Jefferson and Madison
O'Brien John, cor 18th and Douglas
O'Brien Patrick, 805 S 15th
O'Brien Thos, nw cor 7th and Washington, saloon
O'Connell C, 219 N 14th
O'Connell Wm, 610 N 4th
O'Connor John, 1003 S 3d
O'Connor M, 106 N 6th, saloon and restaurant
O'Connor Mrs, 821 E Adams
O'Crowley Daniel, 1102 S 7th
Odam David, 319 N 6th
Odiorne Alfred, 1181 N 3d
O'Donnell Michael, 726 N 8th
O'Donnell P P, 529 ns square, confectionery
O'Donnell John, W Calhoun av e of 609
O'Donnell R H, 728 S 14th
Officer W H, sw cor 4th and N G av
Oglesby M, 1724 E Adams
O'Hara Mrs, 830 E Madison
Ohman K M, 228 E Monroe
O'Hara Mrs Mary, W Calhoun av e of 379
O'Hara E, E Edwards bet 9th and 10th
Oldroyd O H, 1101 S 7th
Oliver Stephen, nw cor 3d and Allen
O'Neil Thos, N 13th bet Jefferson and Madison
Opel Mrs Margaret, 128 West Reynolds
Opel Nicholas, 827 E Mason
Ossenberger Joseph, 14th, bet Jefferson and Madison
Ordway John, 322 N 2d
Orendorff A, sw cor 2d and Washington
Orendorff & Creighton, 501 ns square, attorneys
Ormsbey Geo, 1211 E Jefferson
Orr Joseph, 1223 E Adams
Orr Wm, 554 W William
—11

Ornellas Mary C, 306 N 14th
Osgood F H, 106 es square, boots and shoes
Oswald Geo, 1608 E Capitol av
Oston Olley, 900 E Monroe
O'Toole Fergus, 1124 E Madison
Ott Nicholas, Edwards bet 16th and 17th
Ott John, 23 W Carpenter
Owens Richard, cor 11th and Division
Owen J C, 913 W Jefferson
Owen J P, Adams bet 3d and 4th
Owens Samuel, S 4th bet Washington and Adams

PADDOCK JAS H, 1020 S 7th
    Paine E G, N 9th bet Division and N G av
    Paine Mrs M, 300 S 7th
Paine Henry, 811 E Jefferson
Paine Enoch, W Capitol av bet New and Lewis
Paitrow C M, 310 W Wright
Palmer John, 1124 E Jackson
Palmer, Enterprise bet 10th and 11th
Palmer Dr G W, 223 S 5th, up stairs
Palmer John M, 819 E Mason
Palmer John Mayo, 1119 S 7th
Palmer Edwin E, cor 11th and Cass
Papenhausen Rev Wm, 310 W Edwards
Parker Chas, cor 18th and Adams
Parker John F, 1331 E Washington
Parker Wm, 1420 E Mason
Parker Samuel, 1108 Monroe
Parker A E, E Adams bet 12th and 13th
Parker Rev T A, 406 S 5th
Parks Martha, N 11th bet Washington and Jefferson
Parks Ralph, 919 E Cook
Parks A G, 102 E Madison
Parkerson J J, 822 S 4th
Parr Jas A, S College 1st house s of Wright
Parsons Geo, N 6th bet Bergen and N G av
Pasfield Dr Geo, W Jackson and Pasfield
Pashon Jacob, 1301 E Cook
Patterson O L, 914 E Monroe
Patterson Mrs Sarah, N Klein and Calhoun av
Patterson Robt, 1310 E Washington
Patterson John, nw cor 9th and Carpenter
Patterson Edward, S 1st bet Allen and Vine
Patterson Mrs B, N 4th bet Madison and Mason
Patton & Lanphier, 224 S 5th, attorneys
Patton Jas W, 401 N 4th
Patten M H, ne cor 4th and Scarritt
Pattison John, 1201 E Monroe

Paul Henry, S 8th and Allen
Paul C R, cor 8th and Allen
Paulen D, 516 S 8th, county treasurer
Paulen J, 336 S Doyle av
Paulis Joseph, 413 S 9th
Panit Martin, 1130 N 1st
Payne John H, 721 N 8th
Payne F E, 520 W Edwards
Payran Richard, S Spring bet Allen and Vine
Peaker Thos, N 11th bet Miller and Enos av
Peace Joseph, N 1st n of Miller
Pearl Geo, 1031 S 8th
Peace Wm, N 1st n of Miller
Peet Geo, 13th and Lincoln
Pease Mrs W W, 1005 S 6th
Pease C A, 629 N 5th
Peal Robt, 1314 E Capitol av
Peoples Jas, Washington bet 15th and 16th
Peal Edward, 316 N 5th
Pence Henry, 11th and Kansas—south
Peirce A, 200 N 13th
Pereira A F, 1231 E Jefferson
Pender A, sw cor 7th and Edwards
Pendergrass John, S 3d bet Scarritt and Allen
Pennyman Mrs Mattie, 906 S Spring
Perkins Albert, 403 N 14th
Perkins Mrs Jennie, sw cor 11th and Madison
Perry John, 404 N 15th
Perry H, 1628 E Jackson
Peters John T, 1012 S 7th
Pettibone Mrs Sarah, E Adams bet 8th and 9th
Peterson F J, 13th and Madison
Peterson John, 1427 E Monroe
Peterson J, 231 N 2d
Peterson C, 603 N 5th
Peterson F O, 98 (old no) *W Wright
Pettycuit Frank, Brown n of S G av
Pefley Mary, Kansas bet 10th and 11th
Pfeiffer Daniel, 1220 E Adams
Pfarrer Samuel, 107 N 5th, bakery & restaurant
Phelps Mrs Nancy, 110 W Cook
Phelps H L, 228 E Jackson
Phelps Dr R D, Million's block, dentist
Pheasant S, 443 N 5th
Phœnix Fred, W Mason bet 1st and Klein
Phillips Mrs, cor 15th and Jackson
Phillips Bros, 318 S 6th, trunk factory
Phillips D, 629 N 5th
Phillips M, Jackson bet 15th and 16th

Phillips Robt, 1154 N 5th
Phillips Wm. 1114 N 7th
Phillips Fred, 216 S 5th, merchant tailor
Phillips John L, 226 N 7th
Pierce Mrs E, 219 E Monroe, notions dry goods
Pierce John, 409 W Mason
Hietz Henry, 221½ S 6th, art studio
Pitcher G W, Mason bet 7th and 8th
Pilcher Wm, cor 18th and Cass
Pilcher John, 1316 E Monroe
Pilcher Jep, 828 E Carpenter
Pillsbury W S, sw cor College and W Capitol av
Piper Mary, 707 E Jefferson
Piper Mrs Mary, 1020, N 5th
Piper Chas, 420 W Canedy
Pipers Sophia, 701 E Jefferson
Pirkins W T, 923 N 5th
Pickel Joseph, 122 W Carpenter, grocer
Pinckard Thos, printer, sw cor 8th and Enos av
Pittman J A W, 323 S 5th, photo studio
Pratt T W, S 9th bet Jackson and Edwards
Prather Samuel E, se cor Spring and Charles
Pratt Mrs Essie, 10th and Enterprise
Prentice Wm S, 841 S 2d
Price Thos, 320 W Adams
Price Dr J F, office 309 S 6th
Price George, 821 S 11th
Price Mrs Kate, 305 W Mason
Prickett 330 S State
Prickett Thos G, S 2d, opp State House
Pride W H, 1134 N 4th
Priest John W, E Monroe bet 15th and 16th
Priestman Joseph, 814 E Washington
Pringle A, 425 S 9th
Prichard Joseph S, 933 S 4th
Prouty C W, 932 S 4th
Prouty Charles W, State bet Wash'n and Adams
Place Mrs Lucy, 331 E Madison
Pletz Wm, 1405 E Jackson
Pletz Samuel, 1325 E Jackson
Pletz Samuel & Son, 1001 E Monroe, shoe shop
Pletz Miss, 1118 E Monroe
Pletz E W, 1717 E Capitol av
Pletz Lewis, Jackson bet 16th and 17th
Pletz Ben, 1418 E Monroe
Pletz Wm, 1322 E Jackson
Plowman Richard, 406 N 5th
Planck W H, 328 S State
Poffenberger W C, 928 S 2d

Pogue J F, 619 E Adams, lamp and oil store
Pollard Zack, 1123 E Madison
Porter Sylvester, 1403 E Monroe
Porter Charles, 1509 E Adams
Porter Miss, 631 E Jefferson
Palmier Chit, 413 W Miller
Post Rev R O, N 7th, 4th house n of Enos av
Powell Walter, 1012 E Monroe
Powell James L, S 6th, bet Allen and Vine
Power Mrs, 303 W Jefferson
Power M, 226 S 6th, boot and shoe shop
Power M, 621 E Washington, saloon
Power Charles, 1321 E Adams
Power James, 721 E Washington, saloon
Power M, 1229 E Adams
Purcell James, sw cor 12th and Miller
Puffenbarger G W, 1111 N 7th
Purvines Thos, 10th bet Madison and Mason
Pyle J. R, Carpenter, bet 4th and 5th

QUEENAN PATRICK, 1415 E Monroe
Quigley Richard, sw cor 14th and Cass
Quinn A, 619 E Washington, saloon
Quinn Thomas, 211 E Carpenter
Quinn Michael, ne cor 11th and Mason
Quinn Edward, cor 11th and Kansas
Quinn Joseph, 712 S 14th
Quinn Mrs Mary, 1120 E Mason, groceries
Quint A, 714 S 5th

RABENSTEIN J C, W Jefferson
Rabenstein & Foster, Washington, bet 8th and 9th
Rachm F, 1204 E Monroe
Radcliffe A S, N 6th bet Reynolds and Carpenter
Radican James, 827 E Carpenter
Radcliff J P, 329 N 5th
Rahman Herman, W Calhoun av, w of 518
Rafter Mrs Ellen, 1112 N 3d
Rafferty Michal, 618 E Washington, restaurant
Ragland Mrs V E, 912 S 7th
Raisland A, 418 S 11th
Ragsdale Thomas A, 604 S 6th
Ralph W J, 730 E Monroe
Ralph P, ne cor Williams and Henrietta
Ralph Edward, 614 N 7th
Rames John O, 818 E Mason
Ramstetter Henry, 618 N 5th
Ramstetter Henry, 200 N 5th, Brilliant House
Randall Stephen, 522 S 9th

Ransom J N, 721 S 4th
Ransom Wm, 925 S 5th
Ransom R W, nw cor 10th and Jackson, Wab. Coal Co
Ransom R W, 1237 S 5th
Raps George J, 400 E Adams, saloon
Raps George, 221 W Capitol av
Rapps John W, 418 E Jefferson, bakery
Rathbun Wm, 14.5 E Washington
Raschio Charles, 337 W Mason
Rawson William, 836 S 3d
Rawlings Mrs N K, 103 E Washington.
Rhea James A. 225 S 5th, china store
Ray Joseph, Miller and E G av
Ray Richard, 1707 E Adams
Ray S C, Jackson bet 13th and 14th
Ray Daniel, 1225 S 5th
Ray James, Madison bet 11h and 12th
Raymond Henry, 1500 E Capitol av
Routh Fred, 106 E Mason
Reagan John O, 1142 N 7th
Real James, 1200 E Madison
Regan Edward, 1303 E Capitol av
Reavely Joseph, 121 N 5th, saloon
Redinbo Lucy, Madison bet 9th and 10th
Redlich Herman, 915 E Washington, restaurant
Redmond Margaret, 822 S 14th
Reece John W, 904 E Monroe
Reece J N, sw cor Walnut and Jefferson
Reese John, 1013 E Washington
Reed Charles, 1061 N 5th   •
Reed, A J, 216 N 13th
Reid A, 1146 N 4th
Reeves Thos, S 18th
Reeves M O, 806 E Mason
Reid Daniel, 225 W Capitol av
Reid J A, 923 S 6th
Reed, 1013 S 7th
Reilly Mrs, cor 7th and Douglas
Reilly Chas, 423 E Jefferson, grocer
Reilly John, 212 N 13th
Reilly Wm, 214 N 14th
Reilly Chas, 424 E Jefferson, saloon
Reilly Thos, 429 E Jefferson, grocer
Reilly Michael, 610 W Calhoun av
Reilly Dr, office 215 S 5th, over C H Long's
Reiner Mrs Emma, 216 S 6th
Reisch Joseph, 323 W Madison
Reisch A, 315 N 14th
Reisch Joseph, 516 W Mason

Reisch Joseph, N Rutlege n of Miller
Reisch Joseph & Bro, 627 E Washington, meat market
Reisch Geo, next w of brewery
Reisch Frank, N Rutlege and Colhoun av
Reisch Frank & Broth, brewery Rutlege and Herndon
Reiser S M, 633 N 5th
Reiners Mrs, 1st bet Washington and Jefferson
Regner Chas, S College bet Jackson and Edwards
Remann H C, 402 S 8th
Renzenberger A, 821 E Miller
Renney Jas, W Elliott and Rutlege
Renchber Philip, 11th s of Cass
Rensther Philip, 917 S 11th
Reynolds Mrs Dr W M, 1024 S 6th
Reynolds James, 102? S 15th
Reynolds E S Madison bet 11th and 12th
Rhodes Benjamin, 1st bet Washington and Adams
Rhodes G R, 429 S 9th
Rhodes John T, 824 E Edwards
Rhodes John T & Bro, 728 E Monroe, carpenter & builder
Rhodes Hiram B, 331 W Calhoun av
Roodes Miss E M, Million's block es Square, dressmak'g
Rhodes, 1413 E Jackson
Rheinbarger John A, 918 E Carpenter
Rice G S, 116 W Wright
Rice Henry, 1223 S 8th
Rice Jacob, W Wright
Rice Washington, N 10th bet Madison and Mason
Rice Chas H, 205 S 5th, attorney
Richards Mrs J D, 1210 E Washington
Richardson Jordan, 1307 E Capitol av
Richardson Miss Mollie, 1224 E Mason
Richardson W D, nw cor 2d and Cook
Richardson Howard, 627 W Capitol av
Richardson Harrison, ?08 N 15th
Rickard M F, 909 E Madison
Rickard Jar, E Madison bet 6th and 7th
Rickard Jas F, n 6th bet Jefferson & Madison, wagons
Rickerson Rev F D, 309 N 6th
Ricketts John J, 1215 E Jackson
Rickel Joseph, se cor Klein and Carpenter
Ridgely National Bank, 119 ws Square
Ridgely R M, 1204 S 6th
Ridgely Chas, 631 S 4th
Ridgely N H, se cor 6th and Douglas
Ridgely Henry, 408 S 6th
Ridgeway Samuel, 223 N 6th
Riecks Geo, 217 N 5th, meat market
Riecks Geo, 227 W Calhoun av

Rider John, 1804 E Capitol av
Rieger George, 520 W Mason
Rieser S M, 503 ns Square, The Fair
Reiffer M, 1324 E Monroe
Riffroe Jerry, 704 S 5th
Riley P, W Mason w of Cox
Riordan D, 105 ws Square, clothing
Ripley George C, 731 N 7th
Rippey J M, 412 W Monroe
Rippey J M, 469 E Adams, plumber
Rippon John, old No 88 W Cook
Rippon John, 802 S 4th
Rippon John, se cor 9th and Adams, excelsior foundry
Ripstein Jacob, 513 S 11th
Ripp Chris, 220 W Reynolds
Rites John, 811 E Reynolds
Ritterbusch N, 2d bet Washington and Jefferson
Ritter George, 204 W Jefferson
Ritter George B, 315 W Mason
Ritter Nicholas, 1143 N 3d
Ritter J, 520 N 5th
Ritter Geo & Co, 319 E Washington, barber shop
Ritter Jacob, E Jefferson bet 4th and 5th, barber shop
Roane James F, 1413 E Jackson
Roberts —, 1324 E Jackson
Roberts C D, 502 ss Square, gent's furnishing goods
Roberts James, Mason and 17th
Roberts Charles, N 8th bet Jefferson and Madison
Roberts Charles D, 630 S 6th
Roberts E R, 935 S 6th, circuit clerk
Robinet J S, sw cor 13th and Carpenter
Robertson A H, 517 ns Square, attorney
Robertson Judge A H, cor 5th and Miller
Robinson Mrs, 606 N 4th
Robinson Henson, 520 S 8th
Robinson A R, 415 N 7th
Robinson Thos F, 9th and Enterprise
Robinson Wm T, sw cor 1st and Calhoun av
Robinson John, 716 E Jefferson
Robinson Henson, 114 N 5th, tin store
Robbins A M, 712 S 12th
Rock Mrs James, Jefferson bet 10th and 11th
Rock Patrick, 1202 E Adams
Roderick R, 221 S 5th, book-binder
Roderick Toney, 1117 N 6th
Roderick Richard, N 9th bet Enos av and Lincoln
Rodericks Mrs, Miller bet 10th and 11th
Roderick Jesse, 1125 E Miller
Roderegues Joseph, 623 E Washington, grocer

Roderick John C, E Adams bet 13th and 14th
Rodericks Manuel, 1119 EM iller
Roderick Joseph, 9th and Enterprise
Rodems Peter, 1307 S 12th
Rodam Mrs Geo, 1119 S 11th
Rodam Joseph, S 12th n of S G av
Rogers John A, 1201 E Madison
Rogers H H, 909 E Miller
Rogers Henry C, 1050 N 1st
Rodgers Emery, 1315 E Adams
Rodgers —, E Adams bet 10th and 11th
Rodgers Joseph, 937 S College
Rodgers Edward, 1300 E Adams
Roe E D, 840 N 5th
Rokker Henry W, 309 S 5th, State Printer and Binder
Roll John E, sw cor High and Henrietta
Roll Frank, sw cor High and Henrietta
Roll D E, 813 N 7th
Rollins George H, 1508 E Mason
Rollins Ellis, 1127 E Mason
Role James, Miller bet 9th and 10th
Rooney Mrs H, 121 W Madison
Roman Herman W, bet Canedy and Williams
Rose B B, 1129 S 7th
Rosenmyer A, ne cor 14th and Madison
Rosenmire Mrs Maria, 104 W Jefferson
Rosette John E, 1005 E Carpenter
Rosette J E & Bro, nw cor 6th and Wash'n, attorneys
Rosenwald S, 413 S 7th
Ross Thomas, 815 S 12th
Ross Robert, W Washington w of gas works
Ross Reuben, 115 W Jefferson
Ross Reuben, 419 E Monroe, provisions
Roth Henry, 1223 S 12th
Ropps J W, N 6th bet Carpenter and Miller
Rourke Owen, 1207 E Jackson
Rourke John, 429 S 8th
Rourke P, N 5th bet Reynolds and Carpenter
Rourke Miss Mary, 818 E Carpenter
Rourke Peter, 120 N 13th
Rourke Thomas, E Adams bet 12th and 13th
Rowe John, 118 W Jefferson
Rouse John, cor 12th and S G av
Ruch Jacob, 1037 S College
Ruckel J, 218 S 5th, wall paper and shades
Ruckel E W, N 9th bet Enos av and Lincoln
Ruckel Jacob, 221 W Monroe
Ruffin Henry, Reynolds bet 11th and 12th
Rummel A J, 230 E Wright
—12

Runyon Samuel, 111 W Jefferson
Rupp P, 231 N 4th
Russell John, Lincoln bet 12th and 13th
Russell Chas, N 2d bet Madison and Mason
Ruth R F & Son, 522 ss Square, hardware
Ruth R F, ne cor 6th and Edwards
Rutherford Allice, 719 E Jefferson
Rutz Edward, 607 S 2d
Rubley Samuel, W Mason bet 1st and Klein
Runnix Henry, 825 E Carpenter
Ryan Dennis, se cor Walnut and Edwards
Ryan Chas Jr, 313 S 6th, druggist
Ryan A, 1929 E Washington
Ryan Jas, 1209 E Washington
Ryan Edward, 1104 N 7th
Ryan Dr Chas Sen, 430 S 6th
Ryan A, 14th bet Jefferson and Madison
Ryan——cor 7th and Douglas
Ryan Mrs B, 606 W Monroe
Ryan Mrs, 1531 E Adams
Ryan Jas, 1214 E Madison
Ryan Dr Chas, office se cor 6th and Capitol av
Ryan Jas, Mason and E G av

SADLER WILLIAM, 513 S 9th
  Sadler James H, 1023 E Mason
     Salmon Thomas H, 307 W Reynolds
Salmon Mrs Margaret, 311 W Reynolds
Salmon Thomas, 411 W Mason
Sale A W, 606 S 7th
Salzenstein Mrs, 401 N 5th
Salzenstein & Co, Washington bet 3d and 4th
Sampson Charles, N 3d bet Union and Rafter
Sampson W B, S 8th bet Allen and Vine
Sampson Mrs, sw cor 7th and Mason
Saner Edward, 530 S 9th
Saner Edward G, Cass bet 10th and 11th
Saners Edward, 10th and Edwards, cooper shop
Sanner George, 11th s of Cass
Sanders A D, sw cor Washington and Walnut
Sanders George A, 508 S 7th
Sanders O B & Co, 307 S 6th, grocers
Sanders Oliver B, 500 S 9th
Sanders A D, Leland Hotel, publisher I.O.O.F. Herald
Saunders J R, 604 N 6th
Saunders Ben, 516 S 11th
Sanders & Williams, over 1st Nat. Bank, attorneys
Saunders A H, 124 N 5th, grocers
Saunders A J, 1066 N 5th

Saunders A, 1627 E Mason
Saunders Jacob, 1415 E Adams
Saunders J P, Mason and 18th
Sankey James, 1111 E Jefferson
Sappington Stephen, bet Allen and Vine
Sappington Mrs Mary, 210 W Jefferson
Sappington Frank, se cor Reynolds and Rutlege
Sappington S, 123 N 14th
Sappington David, N 10th bet Madison and Mason
Sarver James, 503 N 5th
Saxer Fred, 817 S 4th
Saxer George, 941 S College
Saylor James B, se cor 4th and Capitol av
Saylor Frank, 102 W Cook
Sayward Mrs D, 554 W Canedy
Saylor John, se cor 4th and Capitol av
Sagey Mrs, W Herndon west end
Sargent E C, 414 E Washington, bakery and restaur't
Sargent --, 1123 E Jefferson
Scanlon Thos, se cor 14th and Adams
Scanlon Lawrence, 1005 S 13th
Scanlon Edward, cor 11th and Cass
Scarritt John, N 7th bet Carpenter and Miller
Scarritt Pat, N 7th bet Carpenter and Miller
Scarritt Pat, nw cor 12th and Carpenter
Scaife T B, 222 E Jefferson bet 2d and 3d
Schafer Mrs M, Reynolds bet 11th and 12th
Schafer John, Madison bet 11th and 12th
Sciffer Adam, 300 W Cook
Schlitt Frederick, E Jefferson, St. Charles hotel
Schaeffer Joseph, 112 N 10th, saloon
Scherginger Frank, sw cor Rutledge and Calhoun av
Schevers H I, N G av bet 11th and 12th
Schevers A, 322 S 4th
Schimenz Martin, 313 W Edwards
Schibeer John A, E Washington bet 9th and 10th
Scharf Mrs S, 350 W Carpenter
Scharf Geo, 1529 E Edwards
Schevers A, 1129 E Jefferson
Schloss A, sw cor 5th and Monroe
Schlipf Fred, 1222 E Mason
Schlotton Wm, 13th bet Mason and Reynolds
Schmidt N, 432 W Carpenter, tailor shop
Schwehart Joseph, W Reynolds
Schloss A, 435 N 5th
Schlitz Joseph, 10th and Washington, Milwaukee beer
Schmidt, M 428 W Carpenter
Schmidt S, 117 N 5th, saloon
Schmidt A, cor 15th and Cook

Schmidt Adolph, 119 W Mason
Schmidt E F, 905 E Reynolds
Schlange Henry, 520 W Monroe
Scholl Geo A, 831 S Spring
Schoeneman John, Western Hotel, 3d and Jefferson
Schoettker J H C, S 8th bet Edwards and Cook
Scholes S D, 618 E Edwards
Schryer——1st bet Washington and Jefferson
Schroyer W J, 124 N 5th, police magistrate
Schroyer J J, 219 W Jefferson
Schroyer Geo, 1129 N 5th
Schryver Richard, 1705 E Adams
Schuchman A, 1420 E Washington
Schuchman A, 1430 E Washington, grocery and saloon
Schuchman Chas, 923 E Carpenter
Schuck Henry, sw cor 9th and Jefferson, lumber yard
Schuck H, nw cor 5th and Allen
Schuckhardt J H, 330 N 4th
Schuenhoff Fred, nw cor 2d and Reynolds
Schutt Fred, 116 W Carpenter
Schultz John H, 910 E Carpenter
Schulz John, cor 7th and Washington
Schneider P, 1415 E Jackson, tailor shop
Schwalm Wm, W Cook bet Spring and College
Schwartz Henry, E Jefferson bet 7th and 8th
Schwarberg G, N 2d n of Union
Schwarberg Edward, 811 E Miller
Schwarberg Gustavus, 811 N 3d
Schwarberg John, N G av bet 1st and 3d
Schwarberg Herman, sw cor Adams and College
Schuler John, 104 W Jefferson
Slowey Frank, 215 S 3d
Scott Dwight, ne cor 1st and Madison
Schmirring Christian, 401 W Miller
Scurry John, 1201 E Adams
Seaman Chas, 432 W Herndon
Seaman Mrs Annie, 915 E Madison
Seaman V, 505 W Hay
Seaman J C, 1323 E Washington
Seaman Chas, 624 S 5th
Sears John V, 1117 N 9th
Sebree Jas S, ne cor Washington and Walnut
Seckers B, 1117 E Madison
Sedgwick Mrs E, 730 E Monroe
Seeders John, 401 N 7th, boarding house
Segin H, 118 E Carpenter
Segin H, alley es square, boot and shoe shop
Seigler John, 224 W Allen
Sekinger Joseph, 923 E Carpenter

Seligman Julius, nw cor Mason and 8th
Seligman Daniel, 439 N 5th
Seligman David, 522 N 5th
Seligman Jacob, N 8th bet Madison and Mason
Seligman Daniel, 318 N 5th, cigar factory
Seligman David, 611 E Washington
Sell A J, 521 N 5th
Sell Frederick, 318 W Capitol av
Sell Miss C, 515 N 5th
Sell A J, 519 N 5th, grocer
Sexton Jerry, 811 S 3d
Sexton John, 410 W Williams
Sexton James, 321 W Jefferson
Sexton Michael, 323 W Jefferson
Sexton Jerry, 11th and Kansas
Seydore —, 844 S 5th
Seymour Joseph, 1216 E Monroe
Shanahan Thomas, 1135 N 5th
Sharp John, 808 E Edwards
Sharpless William, 908 S Spring
Shaughnessy Mrs Mary, S 2d bet Scarritt and Allen
Shaughnessy Edward, 1810 E Capitol av
Shaw James, 922 S 14th
Shaw John, 710 E Reynolds
Shaw George, 228 E Monroe
Shaw Wm, 4th and Washington, saloon
Shaw John S, 9th bet Adams and Monroe, machinest
Shaver Frank, 722 S 12th
Shaw Herman, 1128 E Douglas
Shanley Barney, Madison bet 11th and 12th
Shea Mrs B, se cor Reynolds and Rutledge
Shea Wm, Miller bet 10th and 11th
Shea Mrs, S 15th s of Douglas
Shea John, 1033 N Rutlege
Sheehan Mrs Ellen, 320 W Reynolds
Sheen Wm, 327 W Mason
Shean Thos, 127 W Mason
Shelly M, E Carpenter bet 2d and 3d
Shelly Pat, 1108 E Carpenter
Shephard Wilson, W Jefferson bet 1st and Klein
Shephard Lewis, 114 S Pasfield
Shephard Mrs, 514 E Capitol av
Shephard Moses, N 7th bet Bergen and N G av
Shephard M, 408 E Adams, furniture repairer
Shephard L W, 328 S 8th
Sheehey Edward, 409 W Calhoun av
Sheiry & Baker, 800 S 5th, grocers
Sheiry Mrs E J, S 8th bet Edwards and Cook
Sheridan Pat, 609 N 7th

Sherill John, N G av bet 5th and 6th
Sherwood Mrs, 1224 E Capitol av
Shields D, 804 E Madison
Shields Annie, 1537 E Mason
Shinestein Michael, Jackson bet 13th and 14th
Shinn C W, 714 S 5th
Shinn S, 130 W Madison
Shinn C W, office over 1st Nat Bank, architect
Shipley Wm, 1420 E Capitol av
Shipley Mrs, 1219 E Adams
Shilling Jacob, 348 W Reynolds
Shipman E T, 123 E Carpenter
Shirtliff R, sw cor 2d and Madison
Shirt Ben, 323 W Cook
Shlenn Charles, 1516 E Edwards
Shobaid John, 115 old No N 7th bet Jeff'n and Mad'n
Shockley John, 702 N 2d
Shockley U H, N Klein and Calhoun av
Short Thomas, Jackson bet 16th and 17th
Shrot John, se cor 2d and Carpenter
Shroeder Fred, Jackson bet 14th and 15th
Shrader W W, 405 W Monroe
Shoenbe & Bro, 124 N 6th, saloon
Shutt Wm E, Capitol av bet 7th and 8th
Shutt Thos E, 520 S 5th
Shunk Nick, 424 W Carpenter
Shultz Mrs D, 902 E Monroe
Sibert John, 408 W Mason
Sidner Samuel, 576 W Elliott av
Silva Mrs A, 1223 E Washington
Silva Edward, ne cor 7th and Adams, shoe shop
Silva Edward, 1027 E Madison
Silva Toney, 902 E Monroe
Silva Manuel, 922 S 7th
Silva J, 1027 E Madison
Simmons Frank, S 5th bet Scarritt and Allen
Simmons Mrs, 307 E Monroe
Simmons Geo, 1016 E Monroe
Simmons M F, 710 S 7th
Simpson David, 122 W Jefferson
Simpson G G, 406 E Washington, dye works
Simpson John S, N 8th bet Bergen and N G av
Simpson G T, 619 W Washington
Sims Mrs W V, E Reynolds bet 1st and 2d
Sinnott Edward, se cor 12th and Carpenter
Sinnott Mrs, nw cor Allen and Henrietta
Singleton Clayton, S 3d bet Wright and Canedy
Sives Wm, cor 11th and Reservoir
Sisk Mrs Mary M, 807 E Adams

Slade Jas P, 529 S Spring
Slavins John 1220 S 11th
Slemmons & Co, 929 E Adams, spice mills
Slemmons S A, ne cor 5th and Elm
Smallwood Nathan, N 9th bet Jefferson and Madison
Smatters Mrs J N, N 2d n of Union
Smiley Mrs Jane, 802 E Washington
Smillie Robert, 622 N 5th
Smillie Robt, 726 E Washington
Smyth Miss Margery, 844 S 5th
Smith Thos C, 325 S 5th, undertaker
Smith Fred, sw cor 5th and Scarritt
Smith James, sw cor 10th and Mason
Smith Henderson, 901 S College
Smith Annie, N G av w of Rutledge
Smith Wm H, 214 S 4th
Smith A, S 3d bet Scarritt and Allen
Smith Wm, 1125 E Jefferson
Smith Nicholas, 928 E Miller
Smith Wm T, 613 E Washington, tobacco and cigars
Smith Wm T, 21 N 10th
Smith E S, 1019 S 5th
Smith C M & Co, 524, 526, 528 ss Square, dry goods, etc
Smith F E, 418 E Adams, attorney
Smith Mrs J, Miller bet 9th and 10th
Smith C M & Co, 213 S 6th, grocer
Smith C M & Co, 215 S 6th, druggist
Smith William, 1133 S 7th
Smith E W, 116 E Jefferson
Smith Miss L, Jefferson bet 8th and 9th
Smith A J, 729 W Washington
Smith William, W Miller w of Rutlege
Smith Philip, se cor Madison and Klein
Smith Stephen, 1531 E Cook
Smith James, 948 S 2d
Smith C H, 1127 N 7th
Smith Charles, 13th and Adams
Smith Moses, 914 E Madison
Smith J W, 947 S College
Smith Miss, 1113 E Reynolds
Smith & Hay, 624 and 626 E Washington, w grocers
Smith & Co, 516 ss Square, fancy bazaar
Smith M, 116 N 13th
Smith W F, 418 S Walnut
Smith Mrs A, se cor 14th and Mason
Smith C M, ne cor 4th and Cook
Smith J Taylor, 611 S 4th
Smith L, 1027 S 7th
Snape Joseph, 1012 E Mason

Snape R H, 414 E Monroe
Snell Miss E, 527 ns Square, dress making
Snell L M, 220 S 4th, editor
Snigg John C, 1113 E Adams; attorney, office S 6th
Snively E A, ne cor 6th and Vine
Snodgrass Mrs Mary, 1000 S 2d cor Scarritt
Snodgrass Wm, N G av bet 10th and 11th
Snow Geo, N G av bet 11th and 12th
Snider Joseph, 127 S Doyle av
Snyder Daniel, 544 W Mason
Sollie Wm, Douglas and E G av
Sollers Jas, 607 N 8th
Sollers Mrs, 1404 E Jackson
Sohl G L, 1129 S 12th
Sollomon Robert, 1132 N 6th
Sollomon John, W Herndon west end
Sollomon Peter, N 6th s of N G av
Sollomon John, nw cor 6th and Elm
Sollomon Jacob, 1145 near N G av
Sollomon Robert, sw cor 11th and Miller
Sollomon Thomas, N 4th bet Rafter and N G av
Sommer Nicholas & Bros, 131 W Reynolds, grocers
Sommer M, 215 S Doyle av
Sommer Fred, 630 cor 1st and Miller
Sommer W C, 513 N 5th
Sommer L, 400 E Washington, druggist
Sommer N, 1st bet Carpenter and Miller
Sommer Fred, 311 E Washington
Sommer Louis, S 2d and Edwards
Song Charley Cong, 627 E Adams, laundry
Sonner Miss Tracy, Cass bet 10th and 11th
Sonner A, 1222 E Capitol av
Soost Wm, E Brown bet 13th and 14th
Solle Wm, 1017 E Capitol av
Solon T J, 211 S 6th, boot and shoe shop
Sopinding, cor 15th and Cook
Sourwine Geo, 206 S 5th, barber shop
Sorg Mrs Ellen, 919 E Mason
Souther Louis, 413 W Monroe
Sower Mrs, N 4th near N G av
Sower Andrew, sw cor 10th and Reynolds
Speulda M, W Jefferson bet 1st and 2d
Spath Geo, 422 E Madison
Spear Joseph, W Capitol av and Walnut
Spear & Loose, 907 E Washington, lumber yard
Speakman Mrs G, 435 N 4th
Speaker Henry, E Capitol av bet 10th and 11th
Spence Mrs Mary, S 4th bet Monroe and Capitol
Spence Wm, 917 E Washington, up stairs

Spence John, 425 W Reynolds
Spies A, 231 W Edwards
Spies Toney, 225 W Edwards
Spies A, 226 W Cook
Spies John, 10J7 E Miller
Spook John, 226 W Jackson
Sprague Dr J B, es Square, over Diller's
Sprague Dr, nw cor 14th and Capitol av
Springfield and N W R R office, 121 N 6th
Springfield & Marine and Fire Ins Co, bank es Square
Sprigfield Iron Co, office over Ridgely's Bank
Springfield Commercial College, ne cor Square
Springfield Co-operative Coal Co, 209 S 5th
Springfield Printing Co, 115 ws Square
Springer Mrs, 909 E Reynolds ·
Spring John, 1215 E Adams
Spurway Geo, 115 N 2d
Staley Charles, 1162 N 5th
Stanley John, 305 W Mason
Stanley Mrs Mary, 301 W Mason
Stanléy B F, 83 E Carpenter
Stanton C M, 420 S 5th
Staples Edward, Madison bet 8th and 9th
Stapleworth Frank, 229 W Reynolds
Steward J C, State 2d house s of Washington
Stark —, 1322 E Edwards
Stark & Burgner, 510 E Monroe, laundry
State National Bank, sw cor 5th and Adams
Starne, Dresser & Co's coal office 1st Nat Bank
St Clair O C, 1200 S 4th
St Johns Richard, 1008 E Mason
Stebbins O F, 738 S 5th
Steinritz Charles H, 414 E Adams, harness shop
Steele R C, 424 E Monroe, grocer
Steele Dan, 1147 N G av bet 5th and 6th and
Steilman A, 1025 E Monroe
Steimann Henry, 310 W Reynolds
Steinson Edward, 1119 E Jackson
Stack Edward, cor 11th and Adams
Stack John, 314 N 14th
Stack Miss, 1228 E Capitol av
Stacy Jas D, High and W G av
Stadden Mrs M J, 1006 S 4th
Stafford Mrs P A, 925 E Carpenter
Stafford O N, 718 S 7th
Stahl John, S 10th bet Capitol av and Jackson
Stahl Fred, 421 W Monroe
Stahlen A, E cor 9th and Miller
Staley W sen, 1014 N 5th
—13

Staley Wm, 1050 N 5th
Steiger Chas F, 212 N 2d
Steiger Albert, 302 N 2d
Steiger & Bro, cor 11th and Capitol av, meat market
Steiger & Bro, 10th and Washington, meat market
Steiger & Bro, cor 5th and Jefferson, meat market
Steiger & Bro, cor 5th and Monroe, meat market
Stevenson A, 1535 E Mason
Stevens Geo, 205 N 15th
Stevenson Samuel, 305 W Washington
Stevenson Thos, 905 E Madison
Stevens John H, 425 S 7th
Stevens H A, 110 N 6th, attorney
Stern S, 631 N 5th
Stern Chas, 527 N 6th
Stern Chas, 523 ns Square, clothing
Sterling & Grout, 6th and Washington, attorney's
Stein Adam, 207 W Cook
Steil J P, W Herndon west end
Steinhauster Mrs C, 913 S 11th
Steffan V, 1129 E Adams
Sterniman John, S Pasfield s of Wright
Stock Thomas, 1324 S 11th
Stockdale Wallace, E Allen bet 1st and 2d
Stockdale Mrs, 721 E Mason, boarding house
Stonner Henry, 416 S 8th
Stoneburner Mrs, 11th s of Douglas
Storm John, 125 W Reynolds
Stoneburner William, 617 N 5th
Stoven John, 1120 E Madison
Stott Mrs S M, sw cor 8th and Capitol av
Stock & Dockson, S 7th bet Washington and Adams
Stout Isaac, ne cor 1st and Union
Strott Mrs S R, 642 W Monroe
Strauss William, 425 S College
Strader C, 13th bet Reynolds and Carpenter
Strebel George, 1517 E Cook
Stretch G M, nw cor 3d and Scarritt
Strickland George, 917 S 8th
Strickland Thomas, N 4th and N G av
Strand A, 310 W Reynolds
Strifiler John M, 214 S 5th, ice office
Strifiler J M, 128 W Jefferson
String Simon, 828 E Monroe
Stickley Henry H, E Monroe bet 8th and 9th
Stickel Fred, 172 old No W Carpenter west end
Stillman James, 1723 E Capitol av
Stuart, Edwards & Brown, office State Nat Bank
Stuart John T, 529 S 4th

Stubbs Mrs G, 214 N 8th
Stubbs F N, 1217 E Capitol av
Sullivan Thomas, 801 Barrett
Sullivan Mrs, 810 S 15th
Sullivan Thomas, 10th and Douglas
Sullivan Patrick, 11th s of Kansas
Sullivan John, cor 18th and Capitol av
Sullivan Joseph, N Monroe and 18th
Summergill John, 1112 E Monroe
Supper A, ne cor 4th and Carpenter
Susizie M, 1020 E Reynolds
Sutton G A, office 609 E Monroe, architect
Sutton J C, 516 E Jefferson
Sutton A M, cor 12th and Kansas
Sutton G A, 429 S Spring
Sutton Dan, Madison bet 9th and 10th
Swartz John, 222 E Jefferson
Sweet B F, 1111 N 7th
Sylvester G A, E Washington bet 12th and 13th
Sylvester —, 1219 E Jefferson
Sylvester Joseph, 1324 E Washington

TAINTOR MRS ESTER, 934 W Washington
Talbott Benjamine, cor 6th and Jefferson
Talbott Dr, 220 W Jackson
Tarrant Michael, 333 W Elliott av
Taber Chas W, Madison bet 8th and 9th
Taylor S M, 327 W Monroe
Taylor Daniel, 316 W Wright
Taylor F M, 1404 E Jackson
Taylor Minard, 1104 E Jackson
Taylor Chas A, 517 S 9th
Taylor N, 205 N 7th
Taylor —, W Herndon w of Bond
Tcatena Louis, 317 E Washington, confectioner
Tcneyck Jas, 325 N 10th
Terry W P, 421 W Capitol av
Teufel J, Miller bet 9th and 10th
Teufel C F, 913 E Carpenter
Teal Mrs, cor 11th and Capitol av
Tebbins Mrs Rose, 1102 E Douglas
Tebben Wm, 611 E Washington, saloon
Tiddsbury —, 222 E Washington
Thayer Miss H A, 220 S 4th, day and evening school
Thayer Joseph & Co, 520 ss Square, dry goods
Thisse Miss, Capitol av bet 14th and 15th
Thoma & Reisch, 126 es Square, dry goods
Thoma Frank, 802 S 5th, meat market
Thoma Gregor, ne cor 4th & Adams, Green Tree Hotel

Thoma Henry, 648 N 4th
Thoma Hugo, 416 E Monroe, saloon
Thoma Louis, 201 E Jefferson, saloon
Thoma Frank, 113 E Reynolds
Thomas Wm, cor Douglas and E G av
Thomas M, 12th bet Mason and Reynolds
Thomas Dr W S, 902 E Monroe, laboratory
Thomas Noah, Carpenter bet 11th and 12th
Thomas Carl es Square, sign painter
Thompson A, 218 S 4th
Thompson A, 825 S 12th
Thompson W G, 417 E Jefferson, boarding house
Thompson Chas, S Doyle av and Governor
Thompson T J, 220 S 5th, justice of the peace
Thompson Mrs Mary, 108 W Madison
Thompson Mrs J A M, 1308 N G av
Thompson Thos, cor 12th and Jackson
Thompson Severt, 402 S Doyle av
Thorp Thos, ne cor New and High
Tompkins Nancy, N 8th bet Carpenter and Miller
Thrift Wallace, 824 S 11th
Thrawl W R, 1175 N 9th
Thornton Wm, 211 S Pasfield
Tickor L H, 527 S 8th, county clerk
Tilley J D, 1122 E Jefferson
Tilley J D, cor 10th and Washington, grocer
Tilton Wm, 612 N 6th
Tilton & Reed, S 4th bet Washington and Adams
    farm machinery
Tinan John, 1035 S 3d
Tim Michael, 405 W Reynolds
Tipton Chas H, 1113 N Rutlege
Tipton Mrs, 125 W Jefferson
Tobin J R, N 4th bet Carpenter and Union
Tobin Robt, 1708 E Washington
Tobin Jas, 822 N 7th
Tomlinson N B, nw cor Rutlege and Miller
Tomlinson C W, 1024 S College
Tonges John L, 725 S College
Townsend Dr Justus, 521 S 7th
Todd John, 1808 E Monroe
Todd John H, se cor Allen and Pasfield
Tracy Frank W, 1131 S 6th
Trainer Michael, se cor 10th and Adams
Trapp Dr A H, 403 N 4th
Trapp Fred, 113 ws Square, attorney
Treat S H, 520 S 2d
Trimble Eugene, 218 W Mason
Tripp Mrs M, 517 E Jefferson

Trent Wm, 313 W Wright
Triebel Mrs, 1120 E Monroe
Triley Michael, 1202 E Washington
Traesch M, 109 W Mason
Trotter Geo, W Madison w of Mill
Trotter John, 405 N 1st
Troubles Chas, W Washington w of gas works
Troxell C C, 1008 N 5th
Troxell C C, ne cor 4th and Jefferson, farm machinery
Truax Miss, 220 N 8th
Trutter Joseph, 109 E Jefferson
Trutter Joseph, 103 E Jefferson, meat market
Trutter Joseph, 101 E Jefferson, grocery and saloon
Turner A J, sw cor 11th and Adams
Turner Mrs Annie, S 8th bet Washington and Adams
Turney Mrs Wm A, 924 S 6th
Turley Wm, 901 E Reynolds
Tully Mrs, 831 S 13th
Twohey John, bet 16th and 17th and Cook and Douglas
Twyman R D, 929 E Edwards
Twyman David, cor 9th and Adams
Tyer M A, 1021 E Jefferson
Tyson John R, 805 N 7th

UHLER MRS MARGARET, 631 S 8th
Ulrich E R, cor 12th and Cass
Unverzagt Louis, sw cor 4th and Capitol av
Underfanger John, 934 W Washington
U S Express Co, office 203 S 5th
Unger John, 325 W Edwards
Urban J A, 335 W Carpenter

VAIL THOMAS, Elliott av west
Vail Matthew, 1039 S Spring
Vail Edward, 1129 N Rutlege
Vallage Charles, 1064 N 5th
Van Bergen Mrs C, W Grand av s of High
Vandewalker Charles, 1121 S 8th
Vandercook W, 811 E Capitol av
Vandeventer F, N 6th bet Miller and Enos av
Van Deren Mrs R N, 310 W Capitol av
Vandusen John, N 8th bet Miller and Enos av
Vangundy Daniel, 1731 East Cook
Van Norstrand P, 121 W Jefferson
Van Huff Henry, 913 N 5th
Vanhorn Henry, 322 E Monroe
Vaughn W H, 1216 S 5th
Van Valer James H, E Grand av and Jackson
Vanwey Charles, 830 E Monroe

Vashow A, cor Vine and Pasfield
Vasconselles Mrs, Madison bet 12th and 13th
Vasconselles J J, 1120 E Carpenter
Vasconselles Mrs Lucinda, 408 N 10th
Vasconselles, Joseph, 206 Elliott av
Vonachen Thos, 12th bet Capitol av and Jackson
Vontrice H, 1722 E Capitol av
Vieira Antonio, 1111 E Jefferson
Vieira Manuel, 1009 E Miller
Vieria Boston, Lincoln be 11th and 12th
Vieira Joseph, 119 E Carpenter
Vieira Joseph, Lincoln bet 11th and 12th
Vieira Mary, 410 N 10th
Vierra M, 931 E Mason
Vincent J A, 328 S 7th
Vetter Louis, 704 N 6th
Vetter John, 111 N 5th, grocery
Vogelsang Herman, 407 W Miller
Vogel Leonard, 125 W Carpenter
Volle Mrs Jacob, Pine bet 1st and 3d
Vogel Adam, 107 E Washington
Vogel Thos, 114 E Jefferson
Voght Herman, 204 W Reynolds
Vredenburgh Rector, 227 N 14th
Vredenburgh T D, 1024 S 6th
Vredenburgh Peter, 925 N 7th
Vredenburgh Mrs, 1026 E Jefferson
Vredenburgh Miss T D, 521 N 4th

WABASH COAL CO'S OFFICE, Library building
Wackerle L J, 813 sw cor 10th and Madison
Wackerle L, 1211 E Jefferson
Wadsworth John, 1154 N 4th
Wagoner C C & Co, 301 W Edwards, grocers
Wagoner Chris, 233 W Cook
Wall, Mrs Ellen, Reynolds bet 8th and 9th
Wakefield G H, 217 N 4th, carpenter shop
Wakefield D T, 1st n of Miller
Walden Mrs M, 419 E Jefferson
Walker Mrs R S, 1037 N 5th
Walker E S, nw cor 5th and Vine
Walker Daniel, 223 E Carpenter
Walker Mrs Ludwin, 201 W Mason
Walker E S, 313 S 6th, insurance sgent.
Walker Andrew, N 15th north end
Walker Charles, 212 E Monroe
Walker Henry, 205 N 5th, barber shop
Walker Henry, 217 N 5th, up stairs
Walker N B, S 4th bet Monroe and Capitol av

Wallace Miss Lizzie, S 4th bet Monroe and Capitol av
Wallace Mrs E A, Miller bet 1st and Klein
Wallace Joseph, 609 E Washington, attorney
Wallace Isaac, 225 W Cook, pumps
Wallace Joseph, 524 W Monroe
Wallace Mrs Francis, 400 S 7th
Walsh Mrs Mary, 421 S 9th
Walsh Mrs Mary W, 1145 N 7th
Walsh John, 224 W Mason
Walsh James, E Washington bet 12th and 13th
Walsh Patrick, 410 W Adams
Walsh Martin, S 1st bet Scarritt and Allen
Walsh D W, S 13th bet Jackson and Edwards
Walsh John, 1212 E Washington
Walsh Patrick, cor 11th and Division
Walsh James, 1128 N 6th
Walsh J J, 110 N 5th, harness shop
Walsh J H, 402 E Washington, boarding and saloon
Walters Mrs A, 923 E Cook
Walthers Mrs Fred, 228 W Madison
Ward Jerry, ne cor 9th and Jefferson, lumber yard
Ward James H, 429 W Edwards, Boston Cottage
Ward Mrs, 808 N 5th
Ward W D, 710 N 5th
Ward Jerry, 1016 E Jefferson
Ward Mrs Hattie, 114 S 8th
Ward Neal, 816 E Reynolds
Warner Jacob, N 1st bet Carpenter and Miller
Warner Mrs, 622 N 7th
Warner J J, 129 N 5th, barber shop
Warner W G, 1103 E Jefferson
Warner Charles, 635 W Capitol av
Warner Charles, 212 S 6th, tobacco and cigars
Warren Mrs, Canedy bet Walnut and Henrietta
Warren Phil, 707 S 6th
Warren Thomas, 132 old No S 3d
Warren F G, 1122 E Adams
Watkins Bell, 311 N 10th
Washington Zack, 15th n of Cass
Warsen P A, W Jefferson cor Pasfield
Watson A M, 230 W Jackson
Watson Joel, 306 W Jefferson
Watson Geo T, 1326 E Edwards
Watson Jas M, 1331 E Monroe
Watson Mrs S K, 523 E Jefferson
Watson Seymour, 508 South on W G av
Watts Thos, E Capitol av bet 15th and 16th
Watts R N, 600 W Monroe, meat market
Watts Jas, E Miller bet 9th and 10th

Watts Lewis, 424 N 10th
Water Works office, 614 E Washington
Weaver P A, 226 S Doyle av
Weaver Geo P, 309 W Edwards
Weber H R, 925 S 7th
Weber J P, 721 N 7th
Weber J A, W Edwards bet Walnut and New
Weber Geo R, W Jackson bet College and Pasfield
Weber G F, 1124 S 11th
Weber John R, 1213 S 5th
Weber Mrs, 717 N 7th
Weber Edward, cor 9th and Adams
Webster J A, 926 S 5th
Webster Robert, 408 S 11th
Webster A D, 1310 E Washington
Weeks Walter, 404 S 11th
Wegge J, 1023 E Monroe
Wegener Fred, 216 W Cook
Wegener Mart, se cor 9th and Cook
Weis Fred, W Reynolds w of 1st
Weis Mrs, sw cor 9th and Cook
Weis Fred, 1226 E Washington
Weis Jennie, 423 E Washington, up stairs
Weisenmyer C F, E Washington, harness shop
Weisenmyer Charles, 704 N 7th
Weldon Mrs, S 10th bet Capitol av and Jackson
Weldon Mrs, 1007 S Spring
Weldon J D, 616 W Monroe
Weller Thomas F, cor 10th and N G av
Wells Mrs, 221 E Jefferson
Welton H S, Board Trade rooms 7th and Washington
Wendlandt Dr, 430 S 8th, Lincoln's old home
Wenneburg Henry, 609 Calhoun av
Wenzel W C, 304 N 5th, grocer
Wenzel W C, 823 E Reynolds
West John, sw cor Cook and Spring
West W D, 820 E Edwards
Westenburger G N, 5th and Elm
Wesley John, 923 N 9th
Weisenborger F J, 1030 E Reynolds
Wenez Chris, W Edwards bet 1st and Spring
Weyrauch Peter, 908 E Monroe, saloon
W U Telegraph office, nw cor 5th and Monroe
Wetterer Albert, 215 S 5th, up stairs
Wehno David, 352 W Carpenter
Wetterer Mrs P, 352 W Carpenter
Werhle John, 527 W Hay
Wehrle Leonard, N Rutlege n of Miller
Wehv Mas, 427 W Reynolds

Whaland Mrs, Madison bet 8th and 9th
Whalen John, 325 W Jefferson
Whalen Jas, 815 E Capitol av
Whalen Jas, 126 W Mason
Whalen Thos, 507 W Herndon
Whirty Jas, 920 S 11th, grocery
Wheeler Walter, S 3d bet Scarritt and Allen
Wheeler Thos H, 1125 N 9th
Wheeler Jacob, 1227 S 7th
Wheeler George, 430 W Washington
Wheeler R N, 324 N 7th
Whelton John. Elliott av bet 1st and Rutlege
Wheatlocher Frank, 405 W Mason
Whitcomb J H, sw cor 9th and Edwards
Whitcomb E T, 1021 S 4th
White's saloon, old post office alley w of 6th
White E, 108 N 5th, attorney
White J M, 829 S 4th
White Mrs Martha, sw cor 7th and N G av
White Dick, 216 W Jefferson
White E W, 918 N 6th
White Frank, 529 W Mason
White Albert, 422 N 10th
White Thomas, 1501 E Jackson
White Henry, S 11th
White William, 1017 E Adams
White Matthew, 1404 E Adams
White Wm, 726 and 728 E Adams, carpenter etc
Whitecraft S M, 728 S 7th
Whitecraft Geo W, 731 S 8th
Whitesides Geo, 717 E Washington, boarding
Whitley Rev H C, cor 16th and Capitol av
Whitley Mrs E L, 1031 E Washington
Whittle Richard, 805 S 12th
Whitlock Jas, 1405 E Washington
Whitlock Jesse, 1725 E Capitol av
Whittin L N T, 120 S Walnut
Whipp J W, S 5th South of Capitol av
Whipple J C, 926 S 5th
Whipple John H, 1013 S Spring
Whipple E, 848 S Spring
Wickersham D, 609 E Monroe, grocery
Wickersham Thos, S 11th bet Jackson and Edwards
Wickersham Jas, N G av bet 12th and 13th
Wickersham Mrs M, 1721 E Capitol av
Wickersham D, S 7th bet Jackson and Edwards
Wickham H M, 223 E Washington, coal yard
Wickham H M, 913 N 7th
Wicks A A, 1210 E Edwards
—14

Wicks Mrs, S 12th bet Cook and Douglas
Wielcher Philip, 111 E Carpenter
Wienkoop Mrs Charles, 103 E Washington
Wieties John, reservoir bet 11th and 12th
Wienold Mrs C, 347 W Reynolds
Wieties Jeff, N G av bet 11th and 12th
Wieties Ebert, 116 W Carpenter
Wilber S H, 1122 N 5th
Wilber Frank, 913 S Pasfield
Wilber S H, 712 E Adams, feed and sale stable
Wilcox C, 116 E Carpenter
Wilcox Dr L H, 1005 S 4th
Wilcox Dr L H, office 310 S 6th
Wilcox C F, 5th bet Enos av and Elm
Wiley E R, 103 E Jefferson
Wiley Mrs C, 1229 E Monroe
Wiley Mrs, 722 E Reynolds
Wiley Ebben, 231 W Jackson
Wiley W T, 411 E Monroe, up stairs
Wilkinson A, W Capitol av bet New and Walnut
Wilms Fred, 1203 S 7th
Willett Thomas, N 2d n of Union
Willett S J, 828 E Mason
Willbanks J M, N 8th bet Miller and Enos av
Williams A S, 117 S 8th
Williams Henry, E Madison bet 1st and 2d
Williams Miss, E Adams bet 10th and 11th
Williams George, S 8th bet Adams and Monroe
Williams John, 131 W Madison
Williams Isaac, 1529 E Mason
Williams Harrison, 100 W Jefferson
Williams Susan A, 525 W Mason
Williams John, 300 W Adams
Williams John, 218 S 4th
Williams John, 1712 E Cook
Williams Robert, N Walnut bet Washington and Jeff'n
Williams Lewis W, ne cor Walnut and Allen
Williams M, 214 S 4th
Williams John, 817 Barrett and Cass
Williams Jake, E Washington bet 7th & 8th coal & wood
Williams H, 420 E Washington, undertaker, furniture
Williams D, over C M, Smith's, ss Square, artist
Willis Geo, se cor 10th and Reynolds
Willis P H, E Madison bet 8th and 9th
Willis Edward F, nw cor 10th and Madison
Willis Geo P, 118 S Walnut
Willis John, ne cor Washington and State
Wilson P, E Mason bet 16th and 17th
Wilson J W, 421 W Mason

Wilson H M, N Doyle av
Wilson Thos, 1731 E Adams
Wilson Bluford 906 S 6th
Wilson Edwin A, 406 E Adams, real estate
Wilson T W, Washington w of 1st
Wilson Lucille, 728 E Madison
Wilson Washington, E Monroe and 18th
Wilson A, 1107 E Reynolds
Wilson Geo, N Klein bet Jefferson and Madison
Wilson Mrs, E Capitol av bet 15th and 16th
Wilson Morris, Mason bet 15th and 16th
Wilson J N, 817 S 3d
Wilson Mrs Sarah, S 4th bet Monroe and Capitol av
Wilson Bluford, 227 S 6th, attorney
Wines Rev Fred H, nw cor Monroe and Spring
Wines & Wickersham, 523 E Monroe, attorneys
Wines W B, 525 N 5th
Wing Thos, se cor 10th and Adams
Winston Jas A, 511 S 8th
Winters Daniel, Capitol av bet 10th and 11th
Winters A, 306 W Cook
Winters Mrs, 17th and Monroe
Winters Robt, 1015 S Spring
Witt Wm, 1228 S 12th
Witherspoon——,cor 14th and Cass
Wise——, 1308 South 1.th
Wise Geo, 444 W Herndon w of Brewery
Wise Geo, 1227 E Adams
Withey Geo, cor 11th and Jackson
Withey Wm, 1121 E Monroe
Withey A T, E Monroe bet 11th and 12th
Withey John W, 1211 E Capitol av
Withey Bros, 718 720 722 724 E Washington, wagons
Withrow Sanford, 201 W Allen
Withrow I N, S 9th bet Jackson and Edwards
Witmer D W, 709 E Washington
Wolcott Richmond, over 1st Nat Bank, attorney
Wolgamot John F, old post office alley, saloon
Wolgamot John F, 424 S 5th
Wohlgamuth Dr Henry, 703 S 8th
Wohlgamuth Dr H, office 517 E Monroe
Wolf C & Co, 129 ws Square, hatter and furrier
Wolf Chris, W Reynolds
Wolf August, 379 W Calhoun av
Wolf Chris, 1112 S 7th
Wolf John C, 820 E Reynolds
Wolf A, ne cor Madison and Rutlege
Worth Conrad, 905 W Jefferson
Woods Dan, S 15th s of Douglas

Woods Nellie, 216 N 8th
Wood S, Miller bet 8th and 9th
Woods William, 1108 N 11th
Woods Mrs, 1502 E Douglas
Woods Mrs C, 1000 N 5th
Wood Joseph, 501 S 9th
Woods Miss, cor 10th and Monroe
Wood Coleman, 1704 Capitol av
Woods Robert, 530 W William
Wood E H, 1401 E Jackson
Wood James, W Jefferson w of 411
Wood Seneca, nw cor 4th and Carpenter
Woods James, 318 N.2d
Wood W C, 117 S 2d
Wood Geo A, nw cor 6th and Washington, attorney
Wood William, E Madison bet 2d and 3d
Wood Mrs, nw cor 6th and Washington, up stairs
Woodring L. Mason bet 12th and 13th
Wright James F, 1020 S 4th
Wright Thomas, 402 N 13th
Wright Garner, 902 W Washington
Wright G. Washington bet 3d and 4th, west end store
Wright C H, N 7th bet Madison and Mason
Wright Richard, 1202 E Mason
Wright Presco, W Capitol av bet Lewis and New
Wurster U, 620 E Adams, bakery and saloon

Y ATES MRS E A, W Cook west end
      Yoksch Louis, S 8th bet Scarritt and Allen
      Young W A, N 9th and Enos av
Young Peter, 501 N 7th
Young Peter, 12th and Cass
Young Miss, 5th and Monroe, dress making
Young Bandel, S 12th and Clay
Young Edward, 929 E Monroe
Young Richard, W Jefferson w of Walnut
Young Mrs M, 615 E Monroe, dress making
Young Charles, 802 E Adams
Young James W, 904 S College
York James, 123 N 14th
Y M C A Rooms, 307 S 6th opposite post office

Z AHN FRED H, ws Square, merchant tailor
      Zapf J G, 303 W Madison
      Zeller John, 724 E Edwards
Zeller William, 838 S 2d
Zachelmyer Adam, ne cor Carpenter and Klein
Zumbrook Fred, 110 W Cook

Zumbrook Louis, S 4th bet Vine and S G av
Zimmerman John, sw cor 5th and Jefferson
Zimmerman K B, 900 S 4th

OMISSIONS AND CHANGES.

Mellin N J, 216 S 5th, merchant tailor
Kerlin M, E Jefferson bet 2d and 3d
Compton Peter, 1004 E Washington
Tomlinson Mrs Hannah C, 322 S 6th
Ayers George A, S 8th bet Cook and Douglas
Bourne W H, 418 S 7th
Bischoff W F, State bet Monroe and Washington
Hickox & Striffler, 912 E Adams, Excelsior Mills
Crowley William, 1504 E Washington
Muldoon B, sw cor Madison and 7th, saloon
Robinson William, 1300 E Washington
Johnston Adam Jun, 705 E Washington
Hickey David, E Washington bet 12th and 13th
Floyd J Q A, W Jackson bet College and Pasfield
Day W M, sw cor 9th and Adams, saloon and boarding
Bretz John F, Madison bet 6th and 7th, coal yard
Beaty John, 1705 E Adams
Capitol Coal Co, 811 S 6th n of Leland
Furlong M R, 223 S 6th, attorney
Ives H B, cor 19th and Capitol av, coal yard
Norman A D, 223 S 6th, attorney
McGuire B, E Adams bet 7th and 8th, wagon yard
Palmer Dr G W,, office 310 S 6th
Rupp Philip, 609 E Washington, bakery
Tilton Wm, 413 E Washington, furniture
Williams J, 727 E Washington, coal office
Wilson House, cor 4th and Washington
Elkin Thos C, 329 N 5th
Ward Wm, 120 S 6th, restaurant
Johnston R P, 217 East Monroe, real estate
Condell Dr W R, office 217 South 5th,
Smith & James Drs, office 527 ns Square

SPRINGFIELD BUSINESS DIRECTORY.

Abstracts.

Latham H C & Co, 221 S 6th
Hardin John J, 219 S 6th

Agricultural Implements.

Melton & Logan, 220 N 7th
Post C R & Sons, 7th bet Monroe and Adams
Reed L W & Co, 4th s of Washington
Troxell C C, 4th and Jefferson
Van Duyn G A & Co, 116 N 6th

Architects.

Bell & Hackney, sw cor 5th and Monroe
Bullard S A, 526 ss Square
Helmle George H, 430 S 5th
Shinn C W, over State National Bank

Artist.

Williams Dennis, 528 ss Square

Attorneys.

Adams L B, 427 E Washington
Barrow John F, 214 S 5th
Bradley & Bradley, 117 ws Square
Broadwell N M, 231 S 6th
Burnett Frank W, 523 E Monroe
Conkling William J, 213 S 6th
Collins & Sprague, 104 S 6th
Crook A N J, 218 S 5th
Dowling James E, 109 ws Square
Edwards N W, 441 S 2d
Emery William P, Leland Hotel
Gill Joseph A, nw cor Square
Greene S H, over 1st National Bank
Gross & Conkling, 226 S 5th
Gunn John H, 125 N 5th

Attorneys.

Hay Milton, over 1st National Bank
Haynes R W, over 1st National Bank
Hazlett & Kane, ws Square
Herndon & Colby, 105 ws Square
Houston W T, 110 N 5th
Jones F, 124 S 5th
Kennedy Jas A, 110 N 6th
King J R H, 215 S 6th
Littler D T, over 1st National Bank
Loomis W E, 427 E Washington
Matheny James H Jr, 102 es Square
McClernand & Keyes, nw cor Square
McGuire, Hamilton & Salzenstein, 215 S 6th
· Murray & Turner, 425 E Washington
Orendorff & Creighton, 501 ns Square
Palmers, Robinson & Shutt, 216 S 5th
Patton & Lanphier, 224 S 5th
Rice & Trapp, Court House
Robertson & Maxwell, 517 ns Square
Rosette John E, over Beal's drug store
Rosette Lous, over Beal's drug store
Sanders & Williams, over 1st National Bank
Scholes & Mather, 227 S 6th
Scott J B, 227 S 6th
Smith F E, 418 E Adams
Snigg John C, 220 S 6th
Sterling & Grout, ne cor 6th and Washington
Stevens H A, 110 N 6th
Stuart, Edwards & Brown, over State National Bank
Thompson T J, 218 S 5th
Vincent W A, 217 S 6th
Vredenburgh LaRue, 217 S 6th
Wallace Joseph, over 609 E Washington
White E W, 110 N 5th
Wilson Bluford, 227 S 6th
Wines & Wickersham, 523 E Monroe
Wolcott Richmond, over 1st National Bank
Wood George, over Beal's drug store ns Square

Auctioneers.

Eldridge & Conant, 108 and 110 N 6th
Maxcy James R, 501 E Washington ,

Bakers.

Becker Henry, 918 E Jefferson
Connelly & Co, cor 5th and Monroe
Frey & Hartman, 613 E Monroe

Bakers.

Heimberger L, 100 W Jefferson
Hoff Henry, 922 E Washington
Hofferkamp George, 621 E Monroe
Kreuzkemper H, 413 E Adams
Kunzweiler & Knoppel, 609 E Washington
Long Chas H, 215 S 5th
Merklin L & Co, 207 S 5th
Rafferty M C, 618 E Washington
Rapps J W, 418 E Jefferson
Sargent E C, 414 E Washington
Wurster U, 620 E Adams

Bands.

Goldschmidt's German Band, 404 E Adams
Illinois Watch Co Band, 425 E Washington

Banks.

First National Bank, se cor 6th and Washington
State National Bank, sw cor 5th and Adams
Ridgely National Bank, 119 ws Square
Springfield Marine and Fire Insurance Co, es Square

Barbers.

Bahr H J, 519 E Monroe
Baker D M, 525 E Monroe
Beard Henry, 625 E Washington
Birdson George W, Washington bet 9th and 10th
Edwards Jacob, 605 E Washington
Florville S H, 623 E Adams
Florville William, 118 S 11th
Flynn & Hinton, 402 E Adams
Heimlich J, 204 S 6th
Hender Louis, 206 S 6th
Hicklin H, 617 E Adams
Hoehn William, 416 E Monroe
Killion Thomas, 614 E Washington
Killius Fred, under Leland, south side
Neal William, ne cor 6th and Monroe
Peterson John, nw cor 9th and Washington
Ritter George & Co, 319 E Washington
Ritter Jacob, St. Nicholas, 4th and Jefferson
Saurwein George, 206 S 5th
Walker Henry, 205 N 5th
Warner J J, 129 N 5th

Baths.

Bahr H J, 519 E Monroe
Hoehn William, 416 E Monroe
Killius Fred, under Leland Hotel, south side
Ritter George & Co, 319 E Washington
Ritter Jacob, St. Nicholas, 4th and Jefferson
Warner J J, 129 N 5th

Bottlers.

Bansbach Charles, 525 ns Square
Fischer M A, se cor Lewis and Adams
Johnson & Peterson, sw cor 4th and Carpenter

Billiards

Bekemeyer Wm Sr, 615 E Adams
Doul Mrs E, 413 E Washington
Fitzpatrick J E, 515 ns Square
Gruse Jacob, 617 E Monroe
Hopper & Stevens, 613 E Adams
Kennedy F P, 521 E Monroe
Leland Hotel, 6th and Capitol av
O'Connor M, 106 N 6th
St Nicolas Hotel, cor 4th and Jefferson
Tebben Wm, 611 E Washington
Wolgamot John F, old post office alley

Blacksmiths.

Baehr & Co, cor 2d and Washington
Corey Wm, cor 7th and Adams
Farley John, E Adams bet 7th and 8th
Godenrath John, Monroe bet 4th and 5th
Hall Thos, S 9th bet Adams and Monroe
Hodge Geo, 110 N 8th
James F, cor 9th and Washington
Kennedy Thomas F, 821 E Washington
Kennedy Thomas, 822 E Washington
Kuehn August, cor 1st and Washington
Loeb & Bros, cor Miller and Rutlege
McCauley A, E Jefferson bet 4th and 5th
Shober John W, N 7th bet Jefferson and Madison
Van Horn J, N 2d bet Jefferson and Madison
Thomas Noah, N 7th bet Washington and Jefferson

Bleachery.

McMurphy J G, nw cor 3d and Monroe
—15

Boarding Houses.

Berdikoski Frank, 730 E Washington
Bingham Cook, nw cor 10th and Monroe
Hibbard George, 901 E Capitol av
Fleming Mrs John, 203 E Washington
Johnson John H, S 2d next south of State House
McCabe Mrs M A sr cor Monroe and Spring
Mooney Mrs S P, 331 S 5th
Ohio House, 222 N 5th
Shephard Mrs A, 518 E Capitol av
Stockdale Mrs, 721 E Mason

Boiler Makers.

Drake & Palmer, sw cor 10th and Washington

Bookbinders.

Bokker H W, 309 S 5th, State Binder
Hudson Frank Jun, 221 S 5th
Springfield Journal Co, 315 S 6th
Springfield Printing Co, 115 ws Square

Books and Stationery.

Brown J B, 115 ws Square
Faith Mrs R M, 711 E Adams
Harts P W, 223 S 5th
Simmons Frank, 124 es Square

Boots and Shoes.

Averill Charles G, 111 ws Square
Bartel M J, ne cor 11th and Edwards
Corkery & Triebel, 105 N 5th
Fayart H, 416 E Adams
Harbauer Frank Jun, 412 E Adams
Huntington A, 116 S 6th
Mack R E, 511 ns Square
Myers Frank, 513 ns Square
Ordway Walter, 517 ns Square
Osgood F H, 106 S 6th
Shrader W W, 518 ss Square
Smith C M & Co, 528 ss Square

Brewers.

Reisch Frank & Bros, Herndon and Rutlege

Brokers.

Wilson Edwin A, 406 E Adams
Latham & Souther, 221 S 6th
Maxey James R, 501 ns Square

Brick Manufacturers.

Bretz John, east end of Jackson
Doerfler John & Co, office 221 S th
Doerfler John A & Sons, east.end of Cook
Kloppenburg A, cor N and W Grand avs
Lauterbach John, north of Lincoln Park
Mester Harmon, near Fair grounds
McCarthy C, north end of 1st
Selige H, west end of Jefferson

Broom Makers.

Brown James M, 918 E Monroe
Gall G, 315 W Madison
Seymour Joseph, 1027 E Monroe

Business College.

Bogardus S, nw cor 6th and Washington

Carpenters and Builders.

Beam John C, Capitol av bet 4th and 5th
Buck & McKee, cor 11th and Monroe
Bettinghaus H, 210 N 5th
Brown E F, 1426 E Monroe
Cassett Charles M, cor 3d and Monroe
Conway Patrick, cor 12th and Jefferson
Corby John, 1402 E Jackson
Grossman Peter, N 9th cor Mason
Gehlman E F, 217 E Monroe
Haynes A, shop in old post office alley
Hopping D P, 218 E Monroe
Huston & Whipple, 414 E Allen
Mayhew Wm, cor Monroe and 2d
McGrue Thos A, Washington bet 9th and 10th
Morris A, 813 E Monroe
Oliver & Sylvester, alley es Square
Powell Jas, N 6th n of Madison
Rhodes & Bro, 728 E Monroe
Ritter N, 1143 N 3d
Shephard M, 408 E Adams
Shockley U H, 7th bet Washington and Jefferson
Steelman A, Monroe bet 10th and 11th
Wakefield Geo, 117 N 4th
Weller Thos, 6th and Jefferson
White Wm, 726 E Adams

Carriage Repositories.

Booth & McCosker, E Washington e of 8th
Buckley H P & Co, 110 112 114 S 7th
Withey Bros, 8th bet Washington and Adams

Carpets

Bressmer John, se cor 6th and Adams
Bressmer Chas, 126 es Square
Kimber & Ragsdale, 508 and 510 ss Square
Smith C M & Co, 524 ss Square
Thayer & Co, 520 ss Square

Carriage & Wagon Manufacturers

Booth & McCosker, cor 8th and Washington
Myers, Davidson & Henley, ne cor 6th and Jefferson
Rickard Jas F, N 6th n of Jefferson
Withey Bros, 718 720 722 721 E Washington

Carver.

Helmle Wm, 426 S 5th near Jackson

China, Glass and Queensware.

Ferguson B H, cor 6th and Monroe, opp post office
Myers Frank, 513 ns Square
Rhea J A & Co, 225 S 5th

Cigars and Tobacco.

Booth J R, 217 S 6th
Dinkel L, 525 ns Square
Doul Mrs E, 411 and 413 E Washington
Elshoff Herman, 118 S 6th
Fetzer Charles, 513 E Monroe
Hecht R, 103 N 5th
Redlich H, 915 E Washington
Mueller H E, se cor 6th and Jefferson
Shaw William M, 407 E Washington
Schoettker & Gehring, 231 S 6th
Seligman Daniel, 318 N 5th
Seligman David, over 611 E Washington
Smith William T, 613 E Washington
Veitengruber A, 416 E Jefferson
Walther Mrs S, cor 6th and Washington, up stairs
Warner Charles, 212 S 6th

Coal Dealers.

Bretz John F, Madison bet 6th and 7th
Barclay Coal Mining Co, 108 N 5th
Bradish & McCullough, 4th and Jefferson
Black Diamond Mines, south Junction
Springfield Co-operative Coal Co, 209 S 5th
Starne, Dresser & Co, 1st National Bank, east end
Wabash Coal Co, office ne cor 5th and Monroe, up strs
West End Mines, office 423 E Monroe
Wickham H M, 223 E Washington

Clothiers.

Benjamin S, 103 es Square
Hall & Herrick, cor 6th and Adams
Hunter W S, 125 ws Square
Jacobs C, 122 N 6th
Kusel H A, 205 S 5th
Kusel J A, ne cor 6th and Washington
Lange B A, 123 ws Square
Riordan D, 105 ws Square
Rosenwald S, 117 ws Square
Smith C M & Son, 526 ss Square
Stern Charles, 523 ns Square

Confectioners.

Bakrow Mrs R A, 409 E Washington
Connelly Geo S & Co, 5th and Monroe
Fitzgerald J M, 217 S 5th
Graves B S, 224 S 5th
Kreuger S, 219 S 6th
Long Chas H, 215 S 5th
Maggenti Louis, 607 E Washington
Menchini John, 457 E Monroe
Merklin L & Co, 207 S 5th
O'Donnell P P, 529 ns Square
Pfarrer Samuel, 107 N 5th
Redlich H, 915 E Washington
Scatena Louis, 417 E Washington
Wurster U, 620 E Adams
Zimmerman J, nw cor 9th and Washington

Cooper Shops.

Pringle A, 1000 E Capitol av
Saner Edward, cor 10th and Edwards

Dress-making.

Adams Mrs, 820 E Washington
Bennett Mrs E, 122 N 6th
Burgess Ada, 117 N 4th
Crowell Miss V, 229 E Adams
Eagon Mrs L G, 215 S 6th
Gardner Mrs A L, 312 N 5th
Geathard Mrs R E, 809 E Washington
Hamer Mrs L A, 616 S 5th
Rhodes Miss E M, 104 es Square
Smith Miss M E, 107 ws Square
Snell Miss E, 527 ns Square
Young Miss J G, nw cor 5th and Monroe
Young Mrs S J, 615 E Monroe

Dentists.

Babcock S, over Dodd's drug store 5th and Monroe
Burnett J M, 111 ws Square
Davis K B, 217 S 5th
French A W, 522 ss Square
French C G, 526 ss Square
Latham Allen, 223 S 5th
Laughlin F D, 122 N 6th
Patten M H, 305 S 5th
Phelps R W, 106 es Square

Druggists.

Beal W R, 531 E Washington
Brown J B, 115 ws Square
Diller Isaac R, nw cor 5th and Washington
Diller R W, 122 es Square
Dodds R N, nw cor 5th and Monroe
Fisher J S, 305 S 6th
Fleury Frank, 505 ns Square
Harts P W, 223 S 5th
Ryan Charles Jun, 313 S 6th
Schulze John, 630 E Washington
Smith C M, 215 S 6th
Sommer L, se cor 4th and Washington

Dry Goods.

Bressmer John, se cor 6th and Adams
Furlong James, 128 S 6th
Garland James M, 514 ss Square
Gehrmann C A, 113 ws and 507 ns Square
Herndon R F & Co, 512 ss Square
Herndon R F & Co, nw cor 5th and Adams
Kimber & Ragsdale, 508 and 560 ss Square
Levi Mrs A, 107 ws Square
Reisch & Thoma, 126 es Square
Smith C M & Co, 524 ss Square
Thayer & Co, 520 ss Square

Dyers.

Peel Edward, 316 N 5th
Corcoran W J, 406 E Washington
Feldkamp & Son, 320 E Washington

Elevator.

Elevator Milling Co, 3d and Washington

Elocutionist.

Springfield School of Elocution, etc, 323 S 5th

Express Companies.

American Express Co, 222 S 5th, east side
United States Express Co, 203 S 5th, west side

Fancy Dry Goods and Notions.

Myers Frank, 513 ns Square

Florists.

Doyle M, cor Governor and W G av
Phelps H L, 228 E Jackson
Unverzagt Louis, 3d and Capitol av.

Flour and Feed.

Buckley H P & Co, 110 112 114 S 7th
Day R F & Bro, 404 E Washington
Lawler John, 130 E Jefferson
Lowry John B & Co, 800 E Monroe

Flouring Mills.

Dana L D, cor 7th and Jefferson
Elevator Milling Co, 3d and Washington
Excelsior Mills 912 E Adams
Home Mills cor 3d and Washington
Phoenix Mills, cor 10th and Madison

Foundries and Machine Shops.

Aetna Foundry, cor 2d and Adams
Ide A L, cor 5th and Madison
Rippon John, cor 9th and Adams
Eastman S F, Washington bet 9th and 10th

Furniture.

Barkley Jas H & Co, 219 S 5th
Bisch Philip, 111 N 6th
Crafton & Co, 116 N 5th
DuPleaux Thos, 109 N 5th
Eldredge & Co, 108 and 110 N 6th
Miller J H, 423 E Washington
Priest John W, 519 ns Square
Westenberger G, 417 E Adams
Williams H, 420 E Washington

Grain Dealers.

Ulrich E R, 929 E Adams
Welton H S, Board of Trade Rooms

Wholesale Grocers.

Bunn John W & Co, se cor 5th and Adams
Smith & Hay, 624 and 626 E Washington

Grocers.

Andrew John, cor 11th and Madison
Ballou Geo A, N 6th bet Madison and Mason
Barnes Geo E, nw cor Cook and 9th
Bauman Geo, sw cor Spring and Cook
Bengel Bros, 130 N 5th
Bergschneider Joseph, sw cor 11th and N G av
Bied Mrs Walter, 731 E Adams
Bierbaum John, 1029 E Reynolds
Bittinger J W, 1315 E Capitol av
Booth A, 226 S 6th
Brennan Michael, 901 E Washington
Brewer J H, 229 S 6th
Brewer Wm M, 415 E Monroe
Bruner J E, 210 S 6th
Byerline J G, 115 N 5th
Cantrall M E, sw cor 7th and Madison
Canty Patrick, 1202 E Capitol av
Carmody John, 114 N 6th
Claus A, 427 E Jefferson
Coats A, 1327 E Washington
Cochran H E, 517 E Monroe
Connelly Geo S & Co, cor 5th and Monroe
Conlon P, sw cor Spring and Allen
Dana G S, 511 E Monroe
Day W M, 817 E Adams
DeFrates J & Co, 831 E Reynolds
DeFrates F A, E Jefferson bet 12th and 13th
Doenges A, nw cor Spring and Capitol av
Donahue Thos, 728 E Washington
Doyle M, ne cor 6th and Reynolds
Elsey James, 1130 E Monroe
Elshoff H, sw cor 11th and Cook
Feldkamp Henry, se cor 4th and Carpenter
Fernandes John F, 1201 E Washington
Fernandes M, sw cor Klein and Calhoun av
Fitzgerald J M, 217 S 5th
Fitzpatrick Patrick, sw cor Cook and Spring
Fogarty James, 615 E Washington
Forden J M, 523 E Monroe and 112 N 5th
Fortune L, 706 E Washington
Frey & Hartman, 613 E Monroe
Gaffigan M, 629 E Washington
Goldstein A, se cor 9th and Madison
Good W H, 1156 N 5th
Gordon Geo W, se cor 11th and Jackson
Grant S D, 417 E Monroe
Hampton S C & Son, 223 and 225 S 6th
Handy Thomas, 709 E Adams

Grocers.

Hanlon B, 1207 E Madison
Hardcastle Mrs Joseph, 717 S Spring
Hoffman John, S 4th bet Monroe and Capitol av
Howey Thomas, 1031 E Capitol av
Howey Preston, ne cor 7th and Mason
Huelsman F, 1401 E Edwards
Ives E R, ne cor 11th and Monroe
Kerns A R, 125 N 6th
Kessberger A, N 1st bet Washington and Jefferson
Keily T J, sw cor 5th and N G av
Kussmaul William F, 931 S 11th
Leary Thomas, 1230 E Washington
Leneger A, 1600 E Capitol av
Maher P, 621 E Adams
Mahoney T, ne cor 11th and Jackson
Maurer J C & Co, 405 E Monroe
Maurer M, 231 W Mason
Mendonsa John F, N 8th, triangle store
Midden H, 630 S Spring
McCutcheon George, 1331 E Adams
McGraw James A, nw cor 4th and Madison
McMurphy George, 230 N 6th
McSherry P, 801 E Monroe
Moore A E & Co, 622 S 8th
Moore & Clayton, 409 E Monroe
Murphy James, 416 E Washington
Myers Patrick, 122 N 5th
Nagel & Diehr, 230 W Mason
Nees Dennis, 231 N 5th
Nolan P, 224 W Jefferson
Parkerson J J, 413 E Monroe
Pickel J, 122 W Carpenter
Quinn Mrs Mary, 1120 E Mason
Quinn Michael, ne cor 11th and Mason
Reilly Thomas, 429 E Jefferson
Reilly Charles, 433 E Jefferson
Reisch A, 100 W Jefferson
Roderegues Joseph, 623 E Washington
Sanders O B & Co, 307 S 6th
Saunders A H, 124 and 126 N 5th
Schuchman A, 1430 E Washington
Schuenhoff Lizzie, nw cor 2d and Raynolds
Sell A J, 519 N 5th
Sheiry & Baker, 800 S 5th
Smith C M & Co, 213 S 6th
Solle Wm, 1017 E Capitol av
Sommer Henry, 131 W Reynolds
—16

Grocers.

Steel R C, 422 and 424 E Monroe
Tilley J D, cor 10th and Washington
Trutter Joseph, ne cor 1st and Jefferson
Vasconselles & Goveia, 1135 N 6th
Vetter John, 111 N 5th
Vieira Manuel, 931 E Mason
Wagoner C C & Co, nw cor Edwards and College
Watts R N, sw cor New and Monroe
Webster Robt, 913 E Monroe
Wenzel W C, 304 N 5th
Whearty Jas, 920 S 11th
Wickersham D, 609 E Monroe
Wright J T, 421 E Washington

Gunsmiths.

Correthers Green, 123 N 5th
Payne F E, 419 E Adams

Hair Goods.

Baker Mrs M, 218 S 6th
Griffith H G, 211 S 5th
Hayes Miss K C, 221 E Monroe
Leroy Clemence, 404 E Adams

Hardware.

Fox B F, 509 ns Square
Hudson & House, 506 ss Square
Miller Wm B, 103 ws Square
Ruth R F & Son, 522 ss Square
Stebbins O F, 101 ws Square

Harness Makers.

Busher J & Co, 622 E Adams
McGuire Thos, 117 N 6th
Odam David, 614 E Adams
Rames John O, 213 S 5th
Steinritz C H, 414 E Adams
Walsh J J, 110 N 5th
Wiesenmeyer C F, 419 E Washington

Hats and Caps.

Buck Fred D, 527 ns Square
Conway & Co, 104 es Square
Roberts C D, 502 ss Square
Wolf Chris, 129 ws Square

Hides.

Bryant J M, sw cor 8th and Adams
VanDuyn G A & Co, 116 N 6th

Hominy Mills.

Illinois Hominy Mills, sw cor 4th and Monroe

Hotels.

Germania House, ne cor 3d and Jefferson
Green Tree Hotel, ne cor 4th and Adams
Jefferson House, se cor 7th and Washington
Leland Hotel, nw cor 6th and Capitol av
Marshall House, cor 7th and Adams
Revere House, nw cor 4th and Washington
Tremont House, 420 E Monroe
Sherman House, sw cor 5th and Jefferson
St. Charles Hotel, 216 E Jefferson
St. Nicholas Hotel, se cor 4th and Jefferson
Western Hotel, sw cor 3d and Jefferson

Ice Dealers.

Bradish & McCullough, N 4th bet Jefferson & Madison
Strifller John M, 214 S 5th

Insurance.

Beach E P, sw cor 6th and Monroe, over Ferguson's
Burlingham E P, same as Beach, up stairs
Carman Wm H, ne cor 6th and Adams
Hawley & Grant, 219 S 6th
Ives Harry W, sw cor 6th and Monroe
McConnell John, 516 ss Square
Walker E S, 315 S 6th

Jewelers.

Armbruster O J, 123 N 5th
Chatterton Geo W Jun, 121 ws Square
Claus A, 104 es Square
Fisher A H, 504 ss Square
Gourley A F, ne cor 6th and Monroe
Hammond J B, 227 S 6th
Maxcy J R, 501 ns Square
Sommer Wm C, 512 ss Square
Speulda M, 209 S 5th

Justices of the Peace.

Chesnut John A, 217 S 6th
Kane Henry B, 108 N 5th
Condell John S Jun, 111 N 6th
Fosselman J B, 115 N 6th
Schroyer W M, 124 N 5th
Thompson T J, 218 S 5th

Lamps, Oils and Oil Stoves.

Pogue J F, 619 E Adams

Laundries.

Kee C, 627 E Adams
Stark & Bergen, 510 E Monroe

Liquors, Wholesale.

Eck Joseph, 120 N 6th
Ensel L S, 220 S 6th
Fixmer John P, 131 E Jefferson
Fitzgerald J M, 217 S 5th
Hehnle C A, 119 N 5th
Mueller H E, se cor 6th and Jefferson
Maurer Charles, 917 E Washington

Livery Stables.

Foster John, Washington bet 8th and 9th
Hofferkamp & Bro, 618 E Monroe
Leland Stables, S 6th opposite Leland Hotel
Little S N & Son, nw cor 4th and Adams
Salzenstein E & Co, E Washington bet 3d and 4th

Locksmiths.

Beet R, 410 E Adams
Cottet J, 206 N 4th
Leroy N & Son, 404 E Adams

Lumber Yards.

Baker William B, 923 E Jefferson
Eielson A, 919 E Monroe
Schuck J H, sw cor 9th and Jefferson
Spear & Loose, Washington bet 9th and 10th
Vredenburgh Peter, 231 E Jefferson
Ward Jerry & Co, ne cor 9th and Jefferson.

Machinists.

Eastman S F and Co, E Washington bet 9th and 10th
Johnson W H, 726 E Adams
Wabash Shops, S 10th

Marble Yards

Baum J, nw cor 4th and Jefferson
Johnston Adam, ne cor 7th and Washington

Masonic Goods.

Hudson Frank Jr, 221 S 5th

Meat Markets.

Bochner Geo, 128 N 5th
Bruestle J J, 11th and Mason
Franz B & Bro, cor 8th and N G av
Franz B, 302 N 5th
Gresch Chas, sw cor 11th and Cook
Hahn L H, 411 E Monroe
Hahn Chas, 627 N Klein
Hegele P, cor 6th and N G av
Maurer A, cor 4th and N G av
Merkle H, nw cor Spring and Cook
Metzger Geo, 516 E Monroe
Metzger Wm, 401 E Monroe
Metzger George, se cor 11th and Adams
Reicks G, 217 N 5th
Reisch Joseph J, 627 E Washington
Steiger & Bro, nw cor 5th and Jefferson
Steiger & Bro, sw cor 5th and Monroe
Steiger & Bro, ne cor 10th and Washington
Steiger & Bro, sw cor 11th and Capitol av
Thoma Frank, 802 S 5th
Trutter Joseph, ne cor 1st and Jefferson
Watts R N, sw cor Monroe and New

Merchant Tailors.

Anderson G W, 322 E Washington
Hall & Herrick, ne cor 6th and Adams
Hunter W S, 125 ws Square
Lundahl B B, 104 es Square
Mellin N J, 216 S 5th
Weldon J D 207 S 5th
Willett, S J, 227 S 6th
Zahn Fred H, 103 ws Square
Hagen M, 627 E Washington
Hagney James, 618 E Adams
Hibbs James M, 328 S 6th
Julian J, E Washington bet 9th and 10th
Mambach William, 118 N 6th
Mayol M, 416 E Adams
McKee Robert, 212 S 6th
Melcher William, 418 E Monroe
Schneider, P, 1415 E Jackson
Troesch M, 403 E Adams
Waldron James, 415 E Adams
Zapf & Haendel, 215 S 6th

Music Teachers.

Celler Mrs Helene, 120 N 6th
Charters Miss N S, 215 S 6th
Fisher E R, 504 ss Square
Gregory Mrs A M, 609 N 5th
Greening T B, S 10th, near Laurel
Hawley Addie, 422 S 5th
Meissner B, 321 S 5th

Millinery.

Gehrmann C A, 113 ws Square 507 ns Square
Hayes Miss K C, 221 E Monroe
Herndon R F & Co, 512 ss Square
Kimber & Ragsdale 508 510 ss Square
Levi Mrs A, 107 ws Square
Mills Miss M E. 528 ss Square

Musical Instruments.

Chatterton Geo W, 121 ws Square
Fisher A H, 504 ss Square
Fisher A A, se cor Square
Myers Frank, 513 ns Square

News Dealers.

Simmons Frank, 124 es Square
Brown J B, 115 ws Square
Harts P W, 223 S 5th
Hudson L A, sw cor 6th and Adams

Newspapers.

Morning Monitor, 615 E Monroe
Illinois State Journal, 315 S 6th
Illinois State Register, 514 E Monroe
Illinois Freie Presse, 415 E Jefferson
Springfield Daily Evening Post, 231 S 6th
Odd Fellows Herald, under Leland Hotel
Staats Wochenblatt, Register building

Notions.

Clements Mrs J H, 924 S 11th
Griffith H G, 211 S 5th
McCarthy Mrs J, 1101 Capitol av
Michael R, 227 S 5th
Pearce E, 219 E Monroe
Rieser S M, 503 ns Square, The Fair
Smith & Bro, 516 ss Square
Wright Garner. 318 E Washington

Notions Wholesale.

McMahon James, 130 N 6th, up stairs
Smith & Bro, 516 ss Square

Nurseries.

McGredy John, 1 mile east on Washington
Doyle Michael, W G av and Governor

Paper Mill.

North Spring and Adams

Painters.

Cook & Co, cor Monroe and 2d
Haughey Thomas J, 408 E Washington
Kimble P F, 421 E Adams
Merkle F X, 210 N 5th
Parker William G, 728 E Monroe
Stack & Dockson, 113 S 7th
Weaver P A, 410 E Jefferson
Zimmerman & Prouty, 427 E Washington
Zimmerman R B & Co, 407 E Adams

Painter and Sign Writer.

Thomas Carl L, over Diller's drug store, es Square

Pension Agent.

Mather Thomas F, nw cor 5th and Washington

Picture Frames.

Barkley James H & Co, 219 S 5th
Simmons Frank, 124 es Square

Photographers.

Anderson L S, over Chatterton's, ws Square
Drenkel Bros, 117 ws Square
German C S, 107 ws Square
Jorns G W, 111 ws Square
Ketchum M D, N 5th south of Madison
Pietz Henry, 221½ S 6th
McNulty F, 404 ss Square
Stroud A, 205 N 5th
Pittman J A W, 323 S 5th

Plumbers.

Hanratty O, 326 S 6th
Hellweg & Snape, 412 E Monroe
Rippey J M, 409 E Adams

Physicians.

Artsman, E, 810 E Monroe
Asbury J M, 514 ss Square
Bolles H O, 511 ns Square
Buck & Matthews, 320 S 5th
Condell W R, 217 S 5th
Davis G W, 517 ns Square
Davis W H, 217 S 5th
Dixon J N, 417 and 419 E Washington
Dresser T W, 511 E Monroe
Gaffney E C, 122 N 6th
Goltra J V, 505 W Monroe
Griffith B M, 225 S 5th
Hall J G, ne cor 2d and Capitol av
Hening T S, 426 S 6th
Hickman W A, 122 es Square
Hughes J S, sw cor 5th and Washington
Jones J A Jun, 1015 S 6th
Jayne William, 418 E Adams
James Lizzie P, 213 S 5th
Kilner George, 406 E Adams
Kreider George N, 313 S 6th
McBurnie W S, under Leland Hotel
Million J L, 106 es Square
Morgan G W, 314 S 7th
Palmer G W, 130 S 6th
Price J F, 309 S 6th
Reilly J W, 215 S 5th
Ryan Charles, 400 S 6th
Ryan Walter, 400 S 6th
Stanley B F, 125 S Spring
Sprague J B, 122 es Square
Talbott F, 220 E Jackson
Smith & Jones, 527 ns Square
Townsend J, 418 E Adams
Trapp A H, 403 N 4th
Vincent John A, sw cor 6th and Capitol av
Wendlandt Gustave, 430 S 8th, Lincoln's old home
Wilcox L H, 310 S 6th
Wohlgemuth Henry, 517 E Monroe

Planing Mills.

Baker W B, 9th and Jefferson
Kikendall J N, cor 9th and Adams

Pumps.

Bittinger J W, 1315 E Capitol av
Ordway John, 419 E Monroe
Witmer D W, 111 S 7th